John Lennon

UNSEEN ARCHIVES

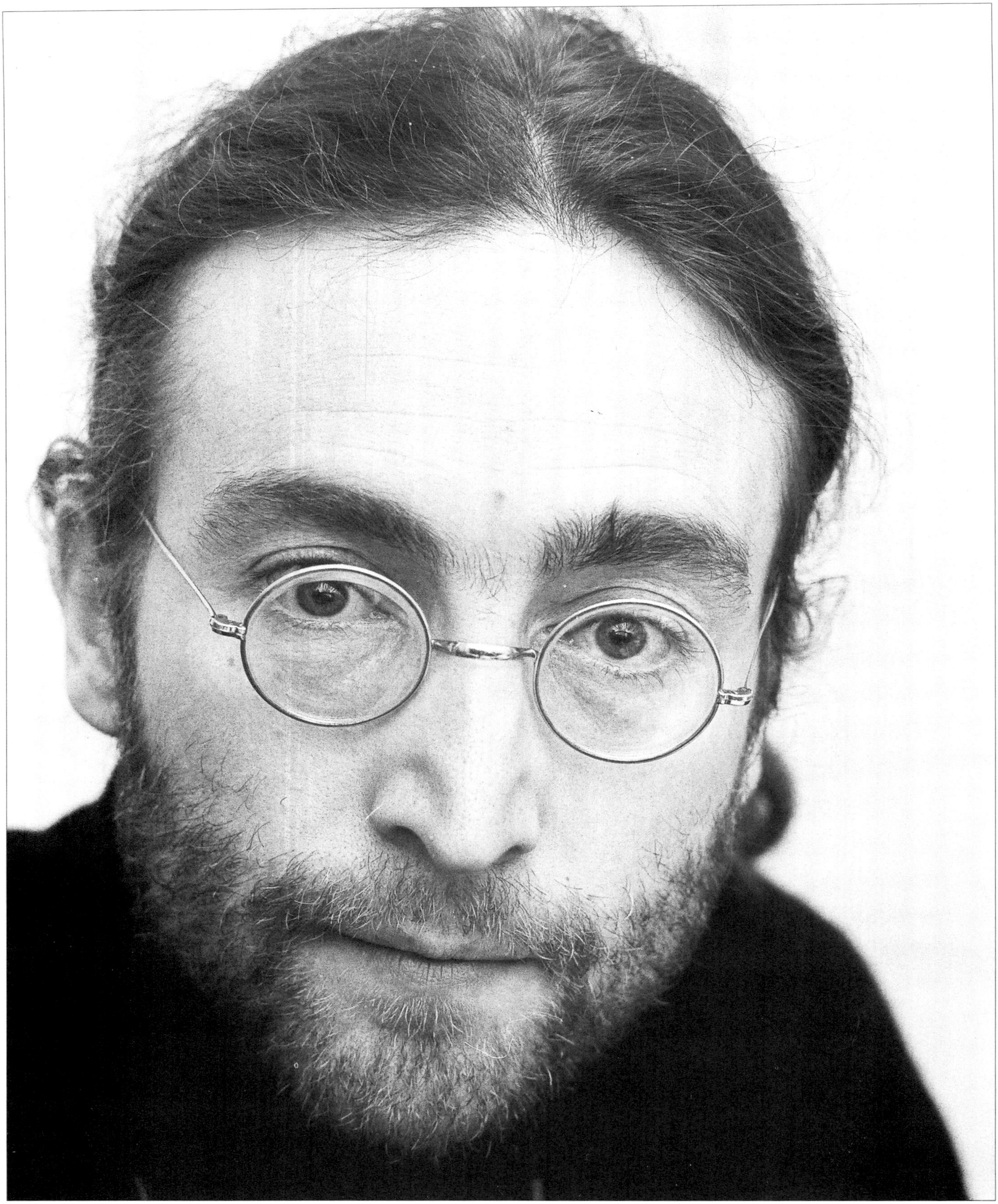

John Lennon

UNSEEN ARCHIVES

MARIE CLAYTON AND GARETH THOMAS

BARNES & NOBLE
BOOKS
NEW YORK

This edition published by Barnes & Noble Inc.,
by arrangement with Parragon

2004 Barnes & Noble Books

M 10 9 8 7 6 5 4 3 2 1

Produced by Atlantic Publishing
Design by John Dunne

ISBN 0-7607-5709-7

Printed in China

Contents

Acknowledgements

The photographs in this book are from the archives of the *Daily Mail*. Additional photographs to complement this fabulous celebration of the life of John Lennon have been provided by the Hulton Getty Picture Collection.

Particular thanks to Steve Torrington, Dave Sheppard, Brian Jackson, Alan Pinnock, Paul Rossiter, Richard Jones and all the staff in the Picture Library at Associated Newspapers without whose help this book would not have been possible.

Thanks also to Jonathan Anderson, Cliff Salter, Richard Betts, Peter Wright, Trevor Bunting, Simon Taylor and John Dunne.

Introduction

John Lennon was the man who brought us The Beatles, and whose energy and commitment to becoming 'bigger than Elvis' was greatly influential in taking them to the heights. He was a man of many contradictions - a superstar who came to hate fame; a singer who didn't like the sound of his own voice; a devoted husband who was often unfaithful. His song writing partnership with Paul McCartney changed the parameters of popular music, and his early prose writing added to the richness and diversity of the English language.

When The Beatles were at the height of their fame, John was known as the thoughtful, intelligent one, celebrated for his sharp wit and swift put-downs. After they broke up, he moved away from commercial music and went on to create a new and exciting career in his own individual way. His relationship with Yoko Ono became one of the great love stories of our times, and with her he developed into both an interesting conceptual artist and an influential campaigner for Peace. After an intense period of experimentation, his music also developed and matured, with his songs reflecting both his philosophy of life and his sharp observation. Despite his talent and commitment to the world of the arts, when his son Sean was born he took five years out of the public eye, dedicating himself to raising his child.

John Lennon: Unseen Archives charts the fascinating life of this complex and charismatic man, right from his Liverpool beginnings to his tragic death in New York. The exciting collection of photographs not only show him performing, but also include candid shots documenting his private life. The photographs are accompanied by detailed captions which give a rounded portrait of the world's first superstar peace campaigner. John Lennon was a phenomenon and his legacy continues to fascinate people even today. He was always a larger-than-life figure, but he has become a true cultural hero of our times.

John Lennon

UNSEEN ARCHIVES

CHAPTER ONE

The Early Years
With love from me to you

John Winston Lennon was a man full of contradictions: often aggressive, with a caustic wit and cutting tongue; against authority and determined to go his own way despite all opposition; but also surprisingly gentle, generous and sometimes deeply sentimental. Much of his complex nature was formed by his troubled and insecure early years - as was revealed in many of his later songs. His mother, Julia, was a cinema usherette when she met and married Alfred Lennon, known as Fred, a ship's steward. Within months of their wedding, Fred was back at sea and although at first he wrote fairly regularly and sent money back, his continual absences severely strained their marriage. Predictably, Fred was at sea when John was born on 9 October 1940 and later his leaves became increasingly erratic and his letters home less frequent. Julia was young and attractive, and she was not prepared to sit at home and wait for a missing husband. A brief affair led to the birth of a daughter, who was quickly adopted, but soon afterwards she met and fell in love with John "Bobby" Dykins, a hotel waiter, and she and the young John moved into his small apartment.

Since Julia was still married the family were horrified and her eldest sister, Mimi, who was married but childless, came to take John away. At first Julia refused to let him go, but when the social services department became involved she gave way and John was whisked off to Mendips, the comfortable home of Mimi and her husband George in Menlove Avenue, Woolton.

For a while John's life settled down. Although she was a strict disciplinarian his aunt had adored him since he was born, and his uncle enjoyed having a surrogate son. John could always rely on Uncle George to play with him, provide encouragement or to bail him out of trouble. He did not lose touch with his mother, as she came to visit him every day. However, in July 1946 Fred Lennon appeared on the scene again, and persuaded Mimi to allow him to take John to Blackpool for the day. He apparently planned to vanish with his son to New Zealand and start a new life, but Julia came rushing after them. The five-year-old John witnessed his parents arguing over who was to have him, and then Fred asked him to choose whom he wanted to live with. It was an impossible situation - he loved his mother, but longed to have his father around. At first John chose Fred, but when Julia left he went running after her in tears. Julia carried him back to the safety of Mimi's house and it was to be many years before John saw his father again.

Julia settled with Bobby Dykins and they had two daughters, Julia and Jacqui. They lived quite near Mimi's house, and John got on well with his two half-sisters and accepted Bobby so he came to visit regularly, but continued living with Mimi. When he started school he did well and, although he was obviously an individual, he stayed out of trouble at first. It was soon after he started at Quarry Bank at eleven that the problems began. Quarry Bank was much more authoritarian, but John quickly decided he did not respect the teachers. It also became apparent that he was very short-sighted, but he hated wearing his glasses so he usually couldn't see the blackboard. On top of all this, in 1955 his beloved Uncle George died suddenly of a hemorrhage. Although John was obviously bright, he lost interest in lessons, began skipping school, swearing and smoking, his grades dropped and he soon had a reputation as a troublemaker. Mimi was worried and upset, but could do nothing to change his attitude.

Meanwhile, John had begun to see more of his mother. Julia was very different to her serious sister - she was headstrong, always smiling, looked down on authority and loved practical jokes. She could play the banjo a little and she taught John a few chords. He soon became seriously interested in music, encouraged by Julia but to the despair of Mimi, who could see no future in it. John and Julia both admired Elvis Presley, and John soon adopted the "teddy boy" look. He also started his own skiffle group, first called The Blackjacks but soon renamed The Quarry Men. It was when The Quarry Men were playing at a church fete in July 1957 that John met Paul McCartney for the first time. Paul came from a musical family and could already play the guitar well, so he was soon invited to join the group.

After leaving Quarry Bank John started at Liverpool College of Art in September 1957. Despite his interest and ability in art he did little better there than he had previously, because now he was determined to let nothing get in the way of his interest in rock 'n' roll. At college John became very friendly with Stuart Sutcliffe, a talented artist, and persuaded him to join The Quarry Men, while Paul introduced George Harrison. It seemed that John had finally found a direction, but he was soon to be struck by another blow. In July 1958, on her way home from Mimi's house, Julia was struck by an automobile as she crossed the road and killed instantly. The death of his mother, whom he had come to regard very much as a kindred spirit, devastated John so badly that he was unable to talk about the loss for many years.

Many students at the college remember John's striking individuality, and girls usually found him very attractive. He had several affairs, but soon became seriously involved with Cynthia Powell. Their relationship seemed unlikely, as Cynthia was from the upscale side of the Mersey, had been strictly brought up and was quiet - almost the total opposite of John - but the attraction was instant and mutual. They soon had a profound influence on each other; John gave up the "teddy boy" look and adopted a more conventional appearance, while Cynthia took note of his obsession with Brigitte Bardot, and proceeded to dye her hair blonde and dress more provocatively.

By 1960 The Quarry Men had changed their name to The Beatles and were developing musically and even earning some money, but the turning point came in August that year when they were offered an engagement in Hamburg. After quickly enrolling Pete Best as drummer, the five of them left for Germany. In Hamburg they met Astrid Kirchherr, who cut their hair into the famous "moptop" style, and in the course of several visits over the next two years the distinctive Beatles sound was developed and honed. Stuart soon left the group, to stay in Hamburg with Astrid and concentrate on his art, but he and John remained close so John was devastated when Stuart died suddenly of a brain hemorrhage. He had lost yet another important person in his life.

By the end of 1961 The Beatles were beginning to make an impact around Liverpool. Local record-store owner and businessman Brian Epstein soon offered to manage them and John accepted on their behalf. In mid-1962, after a great deal of hard work, Epstein achieved a recording contract for the fledgling group with EMI, but EMI's George Martin expressed concerns about Pete Best's drumming. John did not hesitate - telling Epstein that it was up to him to fire Pete, he himself went off to invite Ringo Starr, whom they had met in Hamburg, to join them as drummer instead. The Beatles' line-up was complete. There was also a big change in John's personal life at this time - Cynthia was pregnant so on 23 August the two of them were married in Liverpool.

By October 1962, The Beatles had one record out and were due to appear on their first London TV program, but they were still almost completely unknown outside Merseyside. Throughout 1963 they worked a punishing schedule, which included four national British concert tours, two Scottish tours, one short Swedish tour and numerous one-night shows. They made two LPs, three EPs and four singles, a multitude of TV and radio recordings, and attended many photographic sessions and Press interviews. Their second single was released early in 1963 and, after a rapid climb, hit the number-one spot towards the end of February. At the time The Beatles were on tour supporting Helen Shapiro, but gradually they became the major attraction. The following month brought more joy for John, when Cynthia gave birth to their son, John Charles Julian.

After a grueling schedule, John desperately needed a break, but Cynthia was busy with the new baby. However, Brian Epstein invited him for a holiday in Spain and John was happy to accept. Most people agree that it was entirely innocent - but because of Epstein's homosexuality their time away together started all sorts of rumors about John himself. Things came to a head at Paul's twenty-first birthday party when Cavern Club DJ Bob Wooler made some remark about the holiday. John immediately attacked him, landing him in hospital with a black eye and bruised ribs. The fight became front-page news in the national newspapers; privately John was unrepentant, feeling Wooler was in the wrong, but publicly he was quick to apologize.

In October 1963 a live appearance by The Beatles on the network TV show, Val Parnell's *Sunday Night at the London Palladium*, led to crowds of hysterical fans gathering outside the normally staid theater in London. This caught the attention of the national newspapers, and from then on Beatlemania was in full flow across the nation. When John, Paul, George and Ringo arrived back at Heathrow from a short tour of Sweden a couple of weeks later, they were stunned by the thousands of fans who had gathered in the rain to welcome them back.

Towards the end of 1963, The Beatles were invited to appear at *The Royal Variety Performance*. John was determined to have a dig at royalty at the event, and made his famous and irreverent remark, 'Will the people in the cheaper seats clap your hands? All the rest of you, if you'll just rattle your jewelery.' The year closed with John and Paul being described as 'the outstanding English composers of 1963' in *The Times*. Right from the start they had agreed between themselves that whoever wrote what, everything would carry the names Lennon-McCartney as composers. Neither of them realized just how significant this was to become.

Rocking The Cavern

Opposite: A leather-clad Lennon performing with The Beatles at the Cavern Club in December 1961. Although they had met Brian Epstein the previous month, clearly he had not yet begun to smarten their image.

Above: During an early performance by The Beatles, John and Paul share the microphone as they harmonize in what would become a distinctive style.

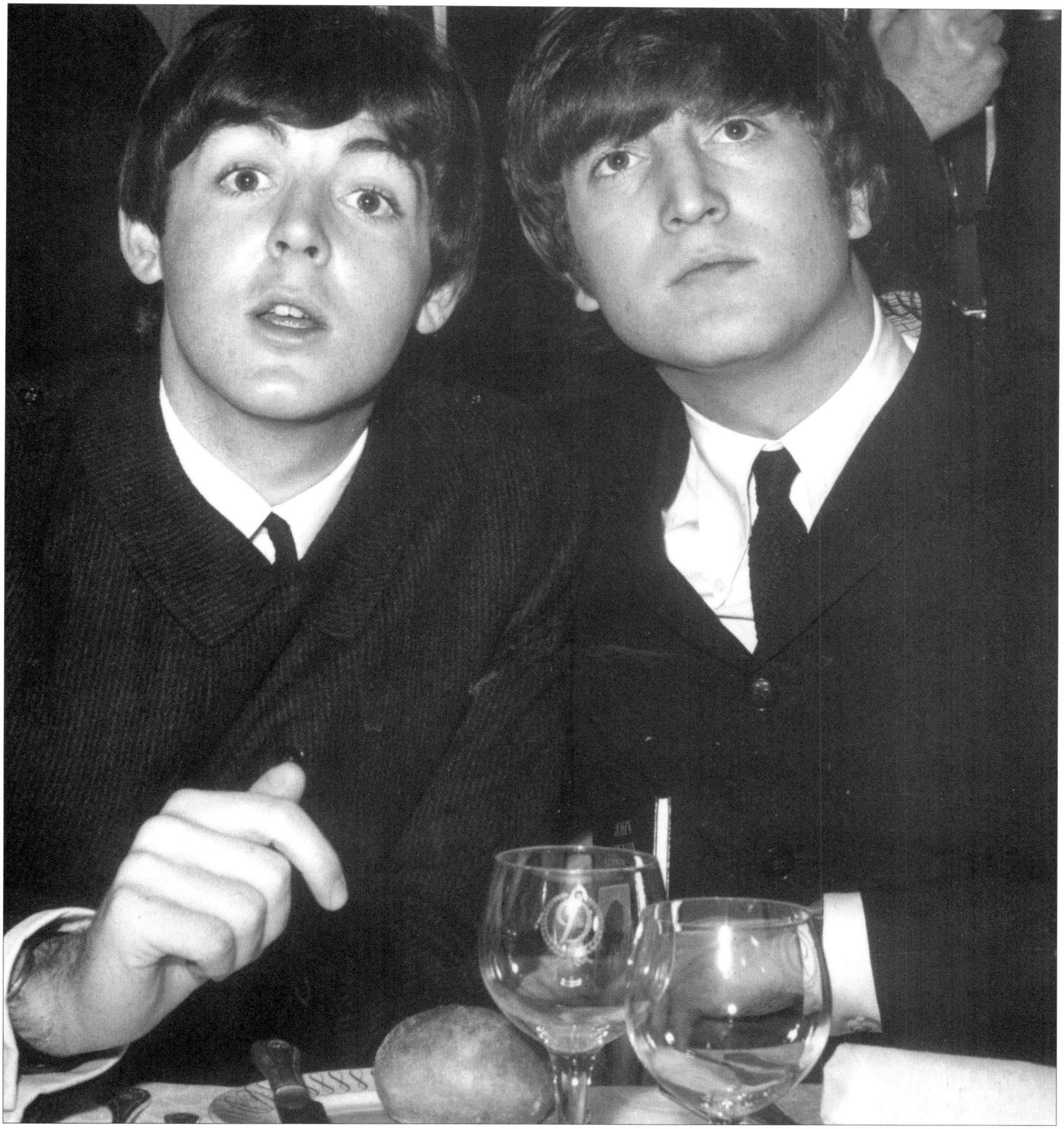

The Beginnings Of Beatlemania

John and Paul display the mop-top haircuts and smart suits that were to become a trademark for The Beatles. 1962 was a turbulent year, full of highs and lows for all four Beatles, and for John in particular. After several grueling stints in Hamburg the four of them were beginning to taste success with radio and the release of their first single, 'Love Me Do'; this was also the year in which John was to lose close friend Stuart Sutcliffe and marry childhood sweetheart Cynthia Powell.

Another time, another place

Throughout 1963 The Beatles worked a punishing schedule, which included four British tours, two Scottish tours, a Swedish tour and numerous single concerts, as well as recording a large amount of new material. They also appeared at many TV and radio sessions, photograph calls and Press interviews.

Above: As Beatlemania took hold, The Beatles had to run the gauntlet of hundreds of screaming fans as they arrived for their concerts. Here they don police helmets as a diversionary tactic in Birmingham.

John's secret

Right: The Beatles gained massive exposure through their national television debut in 1963 on *Thank Your Lucky Stars.* Backstage, John sips tea and relaxes with the rest of the group; he was to make a solo television debut later in the year.

Below: The boys enjoy a meal out. It remains a closely guarded secret that John is married and by now also has a son, Julian.

Celebrated wit

Right: The Beatles jump for joy during rehearsals for the *The Royal Variety Performance* in November, where John was to utter his celebrated witticism, '…those in the cheaper seats clap your hands, the rest of you can just rattle your jewelery'. Apparently, John's comment was something of a compromise, Brian Epstein having pleaded with him to say something less offensive than he had originally intended.

Below: When The Beatles return from a short tour of Sweden in October, their first real European tour, thousands of fans are in London to greet them. Coincidentally Ed Sullivan, with whom Brian Epstein is keen to do business, is on hand to witness Beatlemania for himself.

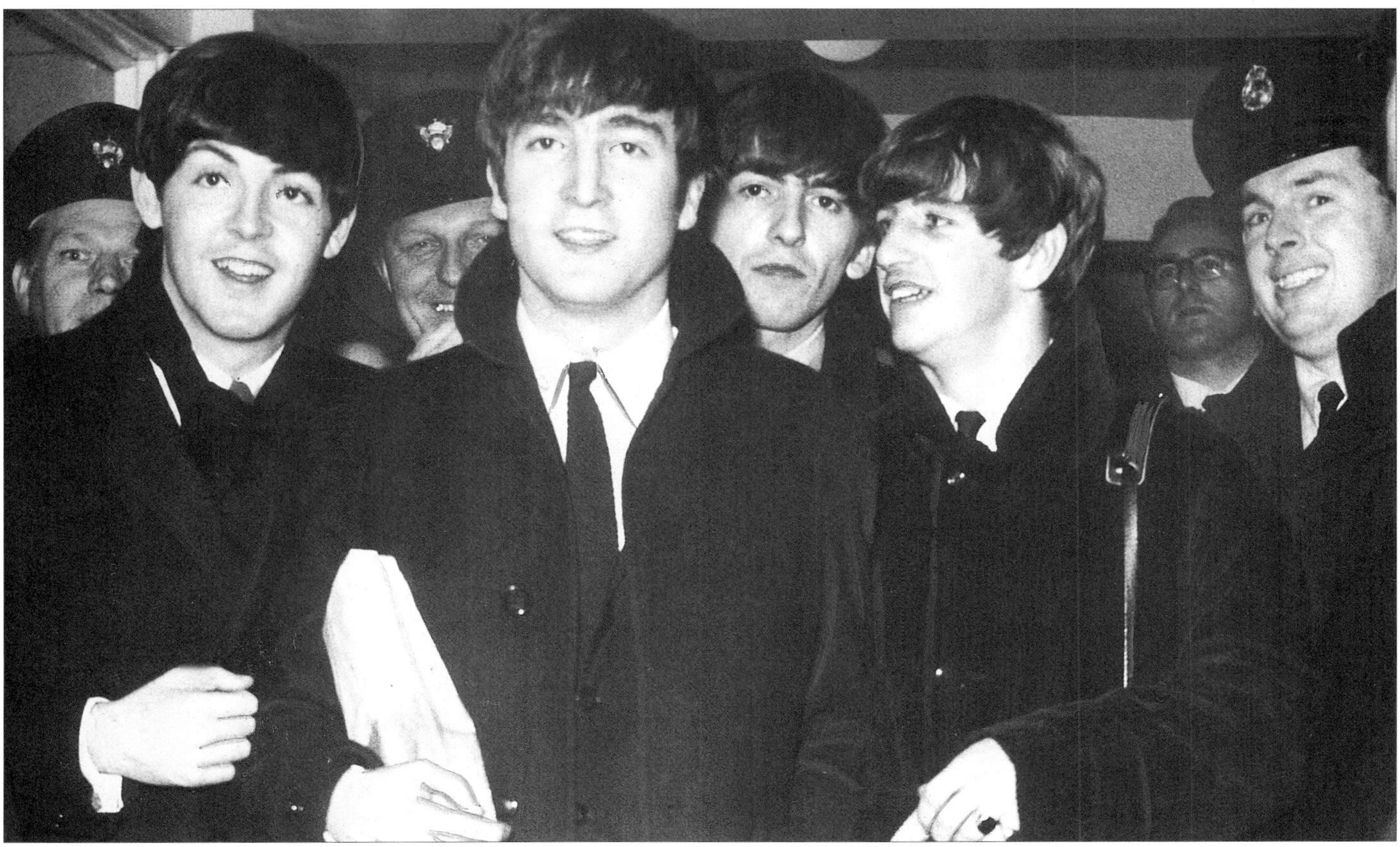

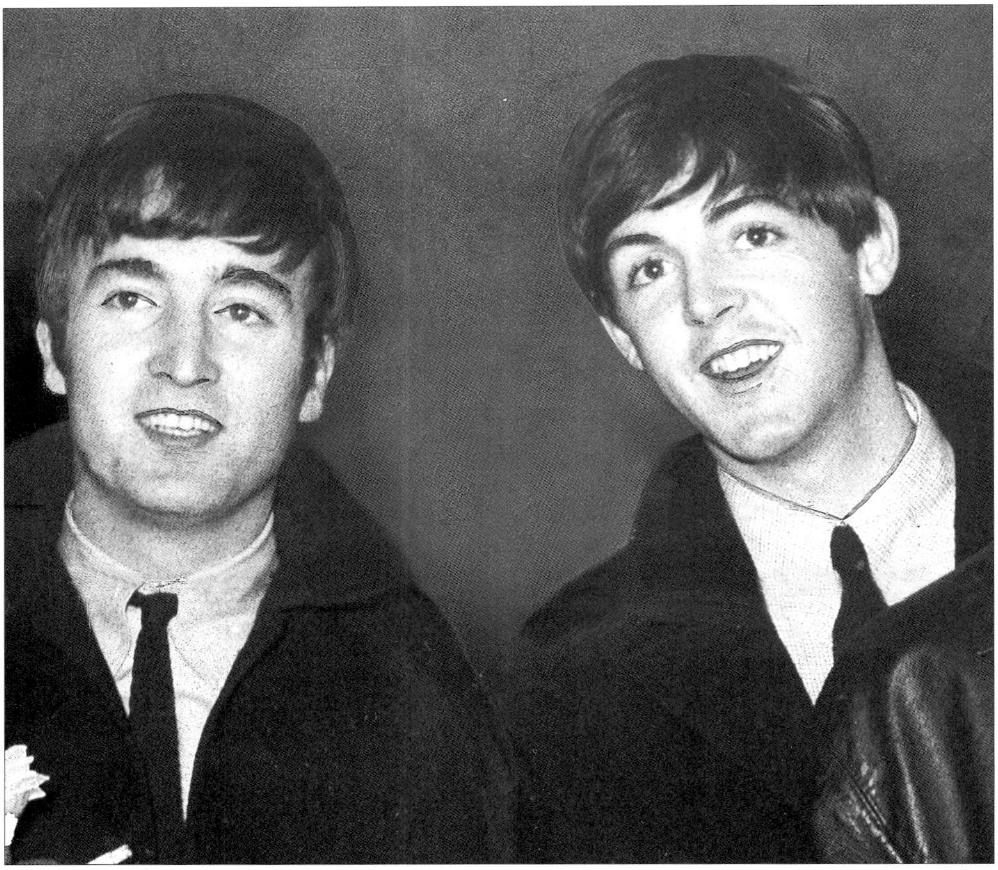

John hits the news

Left and below: By now The Beatles were attracting attention wherever they went, drawing huge crowds and setting trends with their mop-top hairstyles and smart attire. However not all their publicity was so positive; earlier in the year John had hit the headlines in the *Daily Mirror* after beating up Cavern Club DJ Bob Wooler at Paul's 21st birthday party.

Opposite: More television exposure as John plays acoustic guitar when the Fab Four appear on *The Ken Dodd Show*. By the end of 1963 The Beatles had released five singles, three EPs and three LPs.

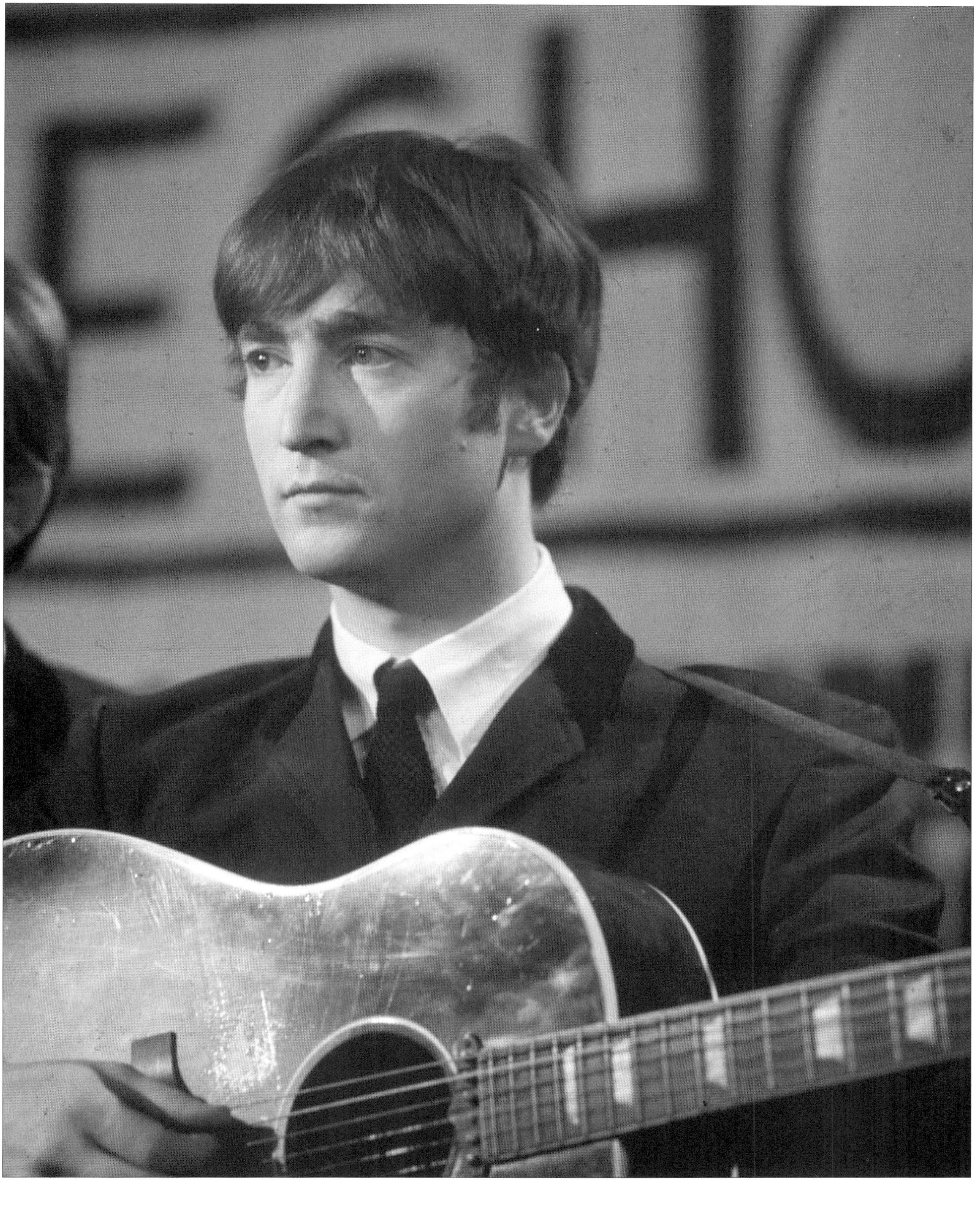

Mersey Beaucoup

Right: John and George leave London Airport for France. Following tours of Britain and Sweden in 1963, the Beatles spent three weeks in Paris early in 1964, performing at the Olympia theater to a somewhat cool reception. On the opening night, John replied to the limited applause with a 'Mersey beaucoup'. During this European hiatus however, The Beatles were informed by telegram of their first US number one - indeed, the first US number one by any British act - with the single 'I Want To Hold Your Hand'.

Above: John pushes his way through the crowds of fans gathered outside the London Palladium.

America Awaits

Opposite: John at London Airport preparing to return to France. John and George came back to London on two occasions for discussions with Brian Epstein during The Beatles' stint in Paris.

Just days after returning from France, and with two albums and numerous singles quickly entering the US charts, The Beatles head off for America, still unsure of the welcome that would await them. WMCA radio in New York kept listeners informed of The Beatles' progress, announcing their departure as '6.30 a.m. Beatle time'.

Right: John in his leather cap, which he seemed particularly fond of wearing, perhaps as a reminder of his 'rocker' days in Hamburg. It prompted one newspaper to ask, '…who dares call a Beatle sloppy?'

Center stage

Above: John and Cynthia wait to board a plane. John was nervous of flying, but often covered up his tension by joking and acting the fool during flights.

Opposite: John takes center stage during a performance. He and Paul shared the singing, although John never liked the sound of his own voice on recordings and often tried to disguise it with special effects.

BEA

CHAPTER TWO

1964
You know I feel alright

In 1964, after consolidating their phenomenal success in Britain, The Beatles were ready to conquer America. No other popular British group had made it big in the States, but John, Paul, George and Ringo were ready to change all that. Their records were already climbing the US charts in February, and soon afterwards the group arrived to appear on *The Ed Sullivan Show* and to give concerts at the Washington Coliseum and Carnegie Hall. Their reception at John F. Kennedy Airport was wildly enthusiastic, as America succumbed to The Beatles in typically wholehearted fashion.

As well as visiting New York and Washington, the boys also spent a few days in Miami, where they not only appeared again live on The Ed Sullivan Show and taped a third performance to be shown later, but also managed a few days of rest and relaxation. Wherever they went, the now-familiar scenes of pandemonium unfolded yet again as American fans went crazy. They also met up with boxer Cassius Clay, who was in Miami preparing to fight Sonny Liston for the World Heavyweight Title. Predictably John pushed his luck with a smart remark to the champ, but luckily Clay saw the joke.

After their brief visit to America, the group returned home to begin work on their first movie, *A Hard Day's Night*, at Twickenham Studios. The storyline was based on incidents from their own lives, a kind of fictionalized documentary of the crazy lives of the world's most famous pop stars. The concept had come from a comment John had made, about how little they had seen of the country during a recent tour of Sweden. Many scenes were shot on location, which was a major logistical exercise, since the fans would quickly gather in their hundreds. For many weeks the movie had only a working title, but after Ringo talked of 'a hard day's night' when recalling a heavy night, everyone realized it was the perfect phrase. The title song, another Lennon-McCartney composition, was sung by John. Although it was made in black and white, the movie was a instant success with the fans and the soundtrack LP quickly went to the top of the UK charts.

Apart from his song-writing, in his spare time John was always writing poems and prose, or doodling. He had already had several articles published and had also written a column under the name Beatcomber in the Liverpool newspaper, *Mersey Beat.* In March 1964, some of his work was published by Jonathan Cape in a book entitled *In His Own Write.* It not only received very complimentary reviews, it also topped the bestseller list in Britain, and in April a Foyle's literary luncheon was held in his honor at the Dorchester Hotel in London. Despite the tradition that the guest of honor should make a substantial speech, John's lasted precisely five seconds. Many guests were disappointed, but he said later that he was scared stiff and did not feel up to speaking for longer.

After four weeks off in May, the longest rest The Beatles had managed for some considerable time, they were ready to begin their first world tour. They were to play thirty-two concerts in nineteen days, across Europe, Australia and New Zealand. The day before their departure disaster struck when Ringo collapsed during a photo-shoot and was rushed to hospital suffering from tonsillitis and pharyngitis. The tour still had to go ahead, so he was quickly replaced by Jimmy Nicol, an experienced session drummer, for the first few dates. Luckily Ringo was well enough to join the tour in Melbourne, and stayed for the rest of the run. Two weeks before they were due to leave, John had phoned his Aunt Mimi and invited her along too, and in New Zealand she made sure he took some time out to visit relatives. John had never met them before, as they had emigrated from Liverpool years earlier to become farmers.

Beatlemania now followed the band wherever they appeared - and not just at concert venues. Whenever the plane stopped for refueling, even in the middle of the night in the remotest of places, crowds of screaming fans would appear from nowhere. Although at first the fame and attention had been flattering, it had quickly gone beyond a joke. It had become a major logistical exercise to get the band to and from the venue in safety, and once inside they had to stay cooped up in their dressing rooms, prisoners of their own fame. On stage, they had to dodge around to avoid being hit by the gifts and candy being thrown by fans and the screaming completely drowned out the sound of the music. John perhaps resented this the most, and was already beginning to regard the live concerts as pointless, since the fans' reaction obviously had little to do with the music. On stage he now often did not bother to sing, just opened and closed his mouth, because he reasoned that no-one could have heard him anyway. Concert tours had become a mind-numbing routine of arriving in town, being smuggled into a venue, performing a show, being hustled into a van for a high-speed getaway to a nearby hotel, and then holing up overnight until it was time to go through it all again the next day. John and the others could not go out in public without being mobbed, their homes were under constant siege from fans and anything not securely fixed down was instantly stolen as a memento.

In July the world charity première at the London Pavilion of *A Hard Day's Night,* attended by all four Beatles, caused scenes of chaos in central London. John disliked crowds - he told several journalists that he felt uncomfortable surrounded by many people. Since he was so short-sighted, and had great trouble with the contact lenses he now wore, he was often unaware of just how many people were around.

A second showing of the movie in Liverpool was followed by a civic reception held for the group in Liverpool Town Hall - a mark of how successful The Beatles had now become. Thousands of people turned out on the day, but John was surprised to find that his old home, Mendips, had become a shrine visited by fans and journalists from around the world. Mimi still lived there alone, but she seemed to take the constant intrusions in her stride. She worried about the fans, and sometimes invited them in for a cup of tea if they looked hungry or cold.

Although John was already a millionaire, he and Cynthia still had no house of their own. At first Cynthia and Julian had deliberately been kept in the background - mainly at Brian Epstein's instigation, as he felt that if the fans knew John was married with a child they would lose interest. However, the secret inevitably got out and it seemed to make very little difference. Their apartment in west London was now constantly surrounded by fans, so in August 1965 John bought Kenwood, a mansion on an estate in Weybridge, which offered slightly more privacy. Since money was no object, he had the whole place decorated, installed an expensive swimming pool and had various other changes made - he ended up spending almost twice what he had paid for the house itself. George and Ringo both lived nearby, but Paul stayed in central London, later buying a house in St John's Wood.

After a few bookings in Britain and another short tour to Sweden, in August The Beatles set off on their first full American tour. It consisted of thirty-two shows in twenty-four cities within thirty-four days so John and the others spent almost the entire time traveling. Again they saw very little of the places they visited, only crowds of rampaging fans wherever they went. However, one important event during the tour was a meeting with Bob Dylan. John admired the American singer's work, and he wrote several songs in the Dylan style. Despite this the two men were too close temperamentally to become great friends - although John did later invite Dylan to his home in Weybridge. Dylan is also popularly supposed to have introduced The Beatles to marijuana. In Hamburg they had experimented with booze and Preludin - a pep pill - but John soon took to marijuana with great enthusiasm.

When The Beatles returned to Britain from America, to the usual hysterical scenes at London Airport, the Prime Minister, Sir Alec Douglas-Home, called them 'our best exports' and 'a useful contribution to the balance of payments'. Only four years previously, John had been a penniless art student; now he was a millionaire, a world-famous pop star, known and sought after by debutantes, dowagers, lords and leading politicians. However, like the other Beatles, he hated being paraded around in front of dignitaries and even more he hated the thought that what had started out as rock 'n' roll was now an industry. As he told a fellow musician at the time, it felt uncomfortably as if he had sold his soul to the devil.

New York, New York

Following a surprisingly warm reception at JFK Airport, New York - including their biggest Press conference so far, where John displayed his sharp wit - The Beatles take the opportunity to look around the Big Apple and John points out some of the sights to Paul.

Right: John and Ringo share the reins during a ride in Central Park, while Paul directs operations. George has obviously thought better of joining in the joint effort.

Below: The cold weather provides the opportunity for a quick snowball fight, Beatle-style.

BEATLES

Crime Prevention

The Beatles went on to perform on *The Ed Sullivan Show*. When it was broadcast, it commanded the largest-ever television audience to date and it was reported that crime fell dramatically during the show!

Left: John turns to face the cameras for a last photograph as The Beatles board the train to Washington, their flight having been canceled due to bad weather.

Below: Sightseeing in Washington - with only a few photographers on hand to record the moment.

Washington

During their time in Washington The Beatles take a trip to see the White House. Despite their growing fame they were still able to move around in public without being mobbed - a situation which was not to last for much longer.

The Washington Coliseum

The Beatles play their first US concert at the Washington Coliseum to around 20,000 people. During the show the boys were pelted with Jelly Babies, following a remark John had made in an earlier interview about George always eating them. The revolving stage gave the audience a great view but was not so easy for the group to handle as they were entirely surrounded.

While The Beatles were still in America, a hastily-made documentary about their visit was shown on UK television. At the same time Beatles merchandise, including mop-top wigs, pillows and scarves, was quickly shipped over to America to tap into the vast new market that had suddenly materialized there.

Left: John in the spotlight.

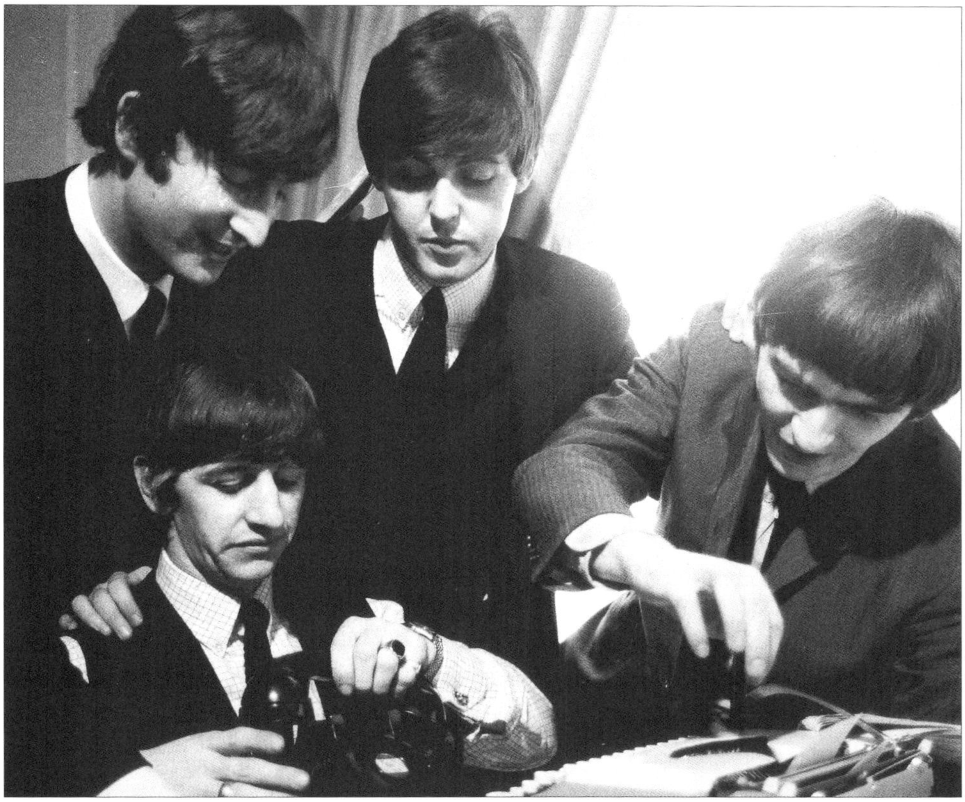

Lennon live

The Beatles followed their first concert with two sell-out dates at Carnegie Hall, where they were greeted by thousands of screaming fans. They had witnessed such hysteria before of course, but perhaps never on such a grand scale.

Left: The Beatles at the Plaza Hotel in New York. Much to the dismay of one executive, the hotel was besieged by hordes of fans - prompting him to offer the group, on-air, to any other hotel willing to take them.

Below: The Beatles themselves took calls from a number of DJs, but unknown to them their conversations were being broadcast on the radio.

When Brian Epstein discovered that John and the others were unwittingly giving away valuable interviews for free, he quickly put a stop to the calls.

John and Cynthia in a 'Twist'

Above: John surveys the crowds of fans gathered outside the Plaza Hotel. During their visit to New York, he and Cynthia visited the Peppermint Lounge, where 'The Twist' dance craze was born.

Miami fashion statement

Traveling to Miami for their second appearance on The Ed Sullivan Show in consecutive weeks, the Beatles took time out to relax, cruising off the coast in a luxury yacht and spending time on Miami Beach, an opportunity afforded them by their somewhat minimal schedule. After only three live concerts and their two appearances for Ed Sullivan, The Beatles had effectively conquered America.

Left and below: Paul wears the captain's cap whilst John still opts for his leather one, despite the glorious February sunshine.

John making waves

Left: Ringo points out a few of the Miami sights to John.

The Beatles enjoy the Miami coastline, running along the beach and paddling in the sea, yet despite these images of relaxation, they are also relishing huge success; their records, including earlier releases, are being eagerly bought across America.

Below: John waves to the cameras with Brian Epstein just behind him as The Beatles make a publicity appearance in the US, shortly before their return to England.

Miami Beach

Although the fans and the photographers were keeping their distance, it would not be long before relaxed and enjoyable scenes like these were a thing of the past as Beatlemania got into its stride across America - and then spread around the world.

The second *Ed Sullivan Show*, which was broadcast live from Miami, was watched by an audience of 70 million. There was also a third show recorded in Miami, which was screened after The Beatles had returned to England.

John pushes his luck with 'the greatest'

Opposite: Performing for a photo call, John looks a real cool dude in his shades and leather cap.

Above and overleaf: Whilst in Miami the Beatles meet the 22-year-old Cassius Clay shortly before his world heavyweight title fight with Sonny Liston. Clay described himself as the greatest, but said The Beatles were the prettiest.

Predictably John pushed his luck with a smart remark to the champ, but luckily Clay saw the joke. Both sides appreciated the publicity generated by the occasion.

GREATEST
218 LBS.
6'3"

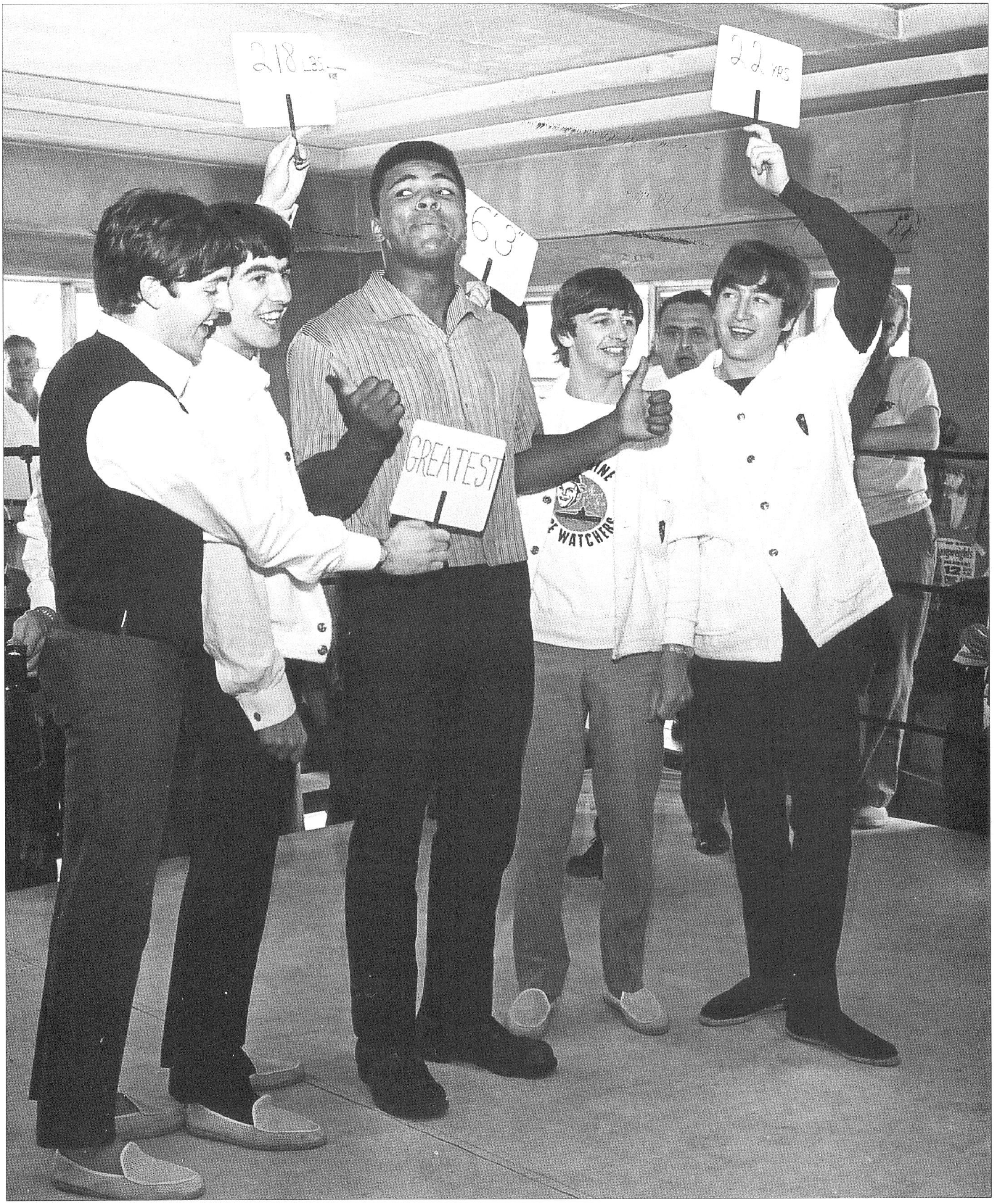
218
6'3"
22 YRS.
GREATEST

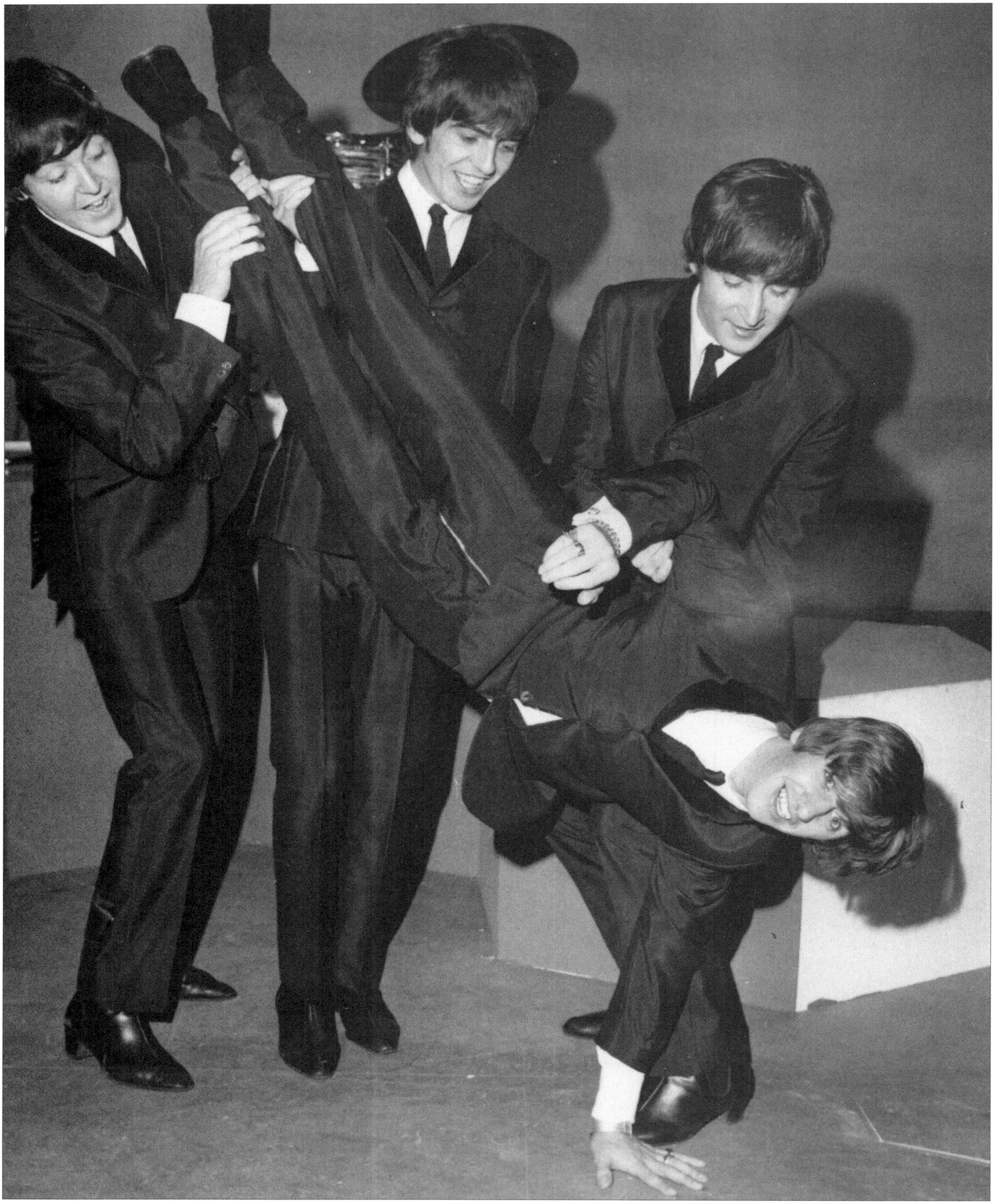

John's Hard Day's Night

The Beatles returned triumphant from America to the usual hysteria and also to praise from the Prime Minister, Sir Alec Douglas-Home, who described the group as Britain's 'best exports'.

Above: The Beatles had once been named 'The Silver Beetles', but now they were to be Beatles of the silver screen. They began to shoot their first movie, *A Hard Day's Night,* less than two weeks after arriving back from America. The concept came from John's response to touring, with The Beatles as prisoners of their own success, living as he put it, from 'a room and a car and a car and a room…'

Pattie Boyd, later to become Mrs Harrison, obtained a part in the movie. She asked them all for their autographs on the first day of shooting, with one notable exception…John, of whom she said she was initially terrified.

Milking it

Opposite: John downs a pint of milk during filming at the Scala Theatre, London.

Above: John and Paul discuss some points of sartorial elegance, with help from George and Ringo. Although John was later to describe acting as 'daft', to begin with he thought that it might enable him to grow in a way that popular music would not allow. However, even his first experience of filming was not to be wholly rewarding. He complained about his lack of input and had to suffer the attention of fans whilst filming - on one occasion he reportedly spent £80,000 whilst rushing through Asprey's to avoid them.

Rickenbacker

Standing on Ceremony

In March 1964 The Beatles were given the Variety Club Show Business Personality of the Year award for 1963, and Carl-Alan awards for Best Group and Best Vocal Record.

Opposite and above: The Variety Club luncheon was held at the Dorchester Hotel and hosted by Harold Wilson, the leader of the Opposition.

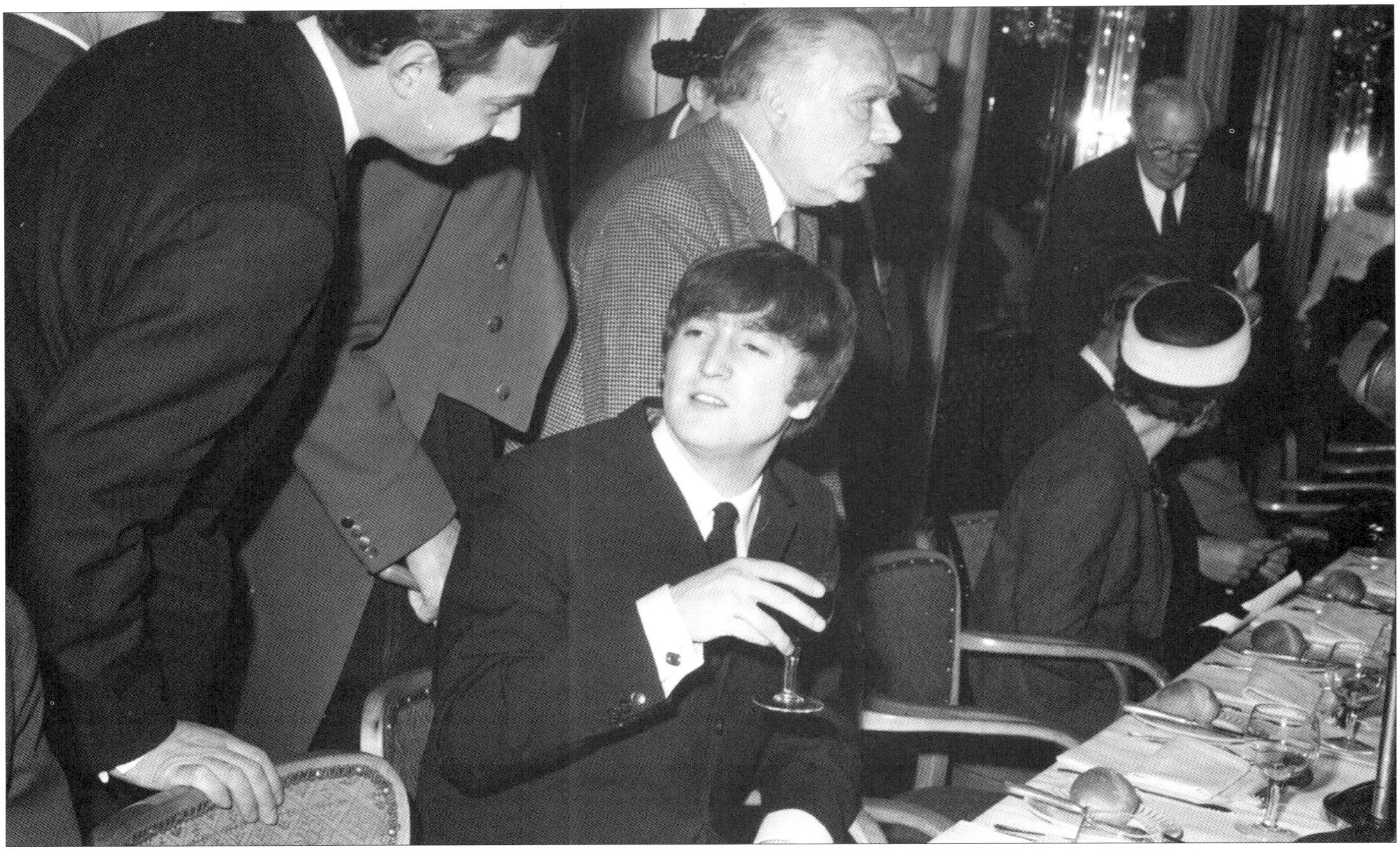

Pepsi

Exhausted

A few days before the Variety Club luncheon, The Beatles had released their latest single, 'Can't Buy Me Love' in the US, but it was not issued in the UK until the day after. By now John and the others were exhausted - all four of them took several weeks off, the longest break they had managed from touring and recording for some time.

Tea with Mary

John takes tea with Harold Wilson's wife Mary at the Variety Club luncheon. Wilson had previously referred to The Beatles as the Conservatives' 'secret weapon' following the comment about exports by the Prime Minister, and he took the opportunity to deny political collusion himself.

Pepsi

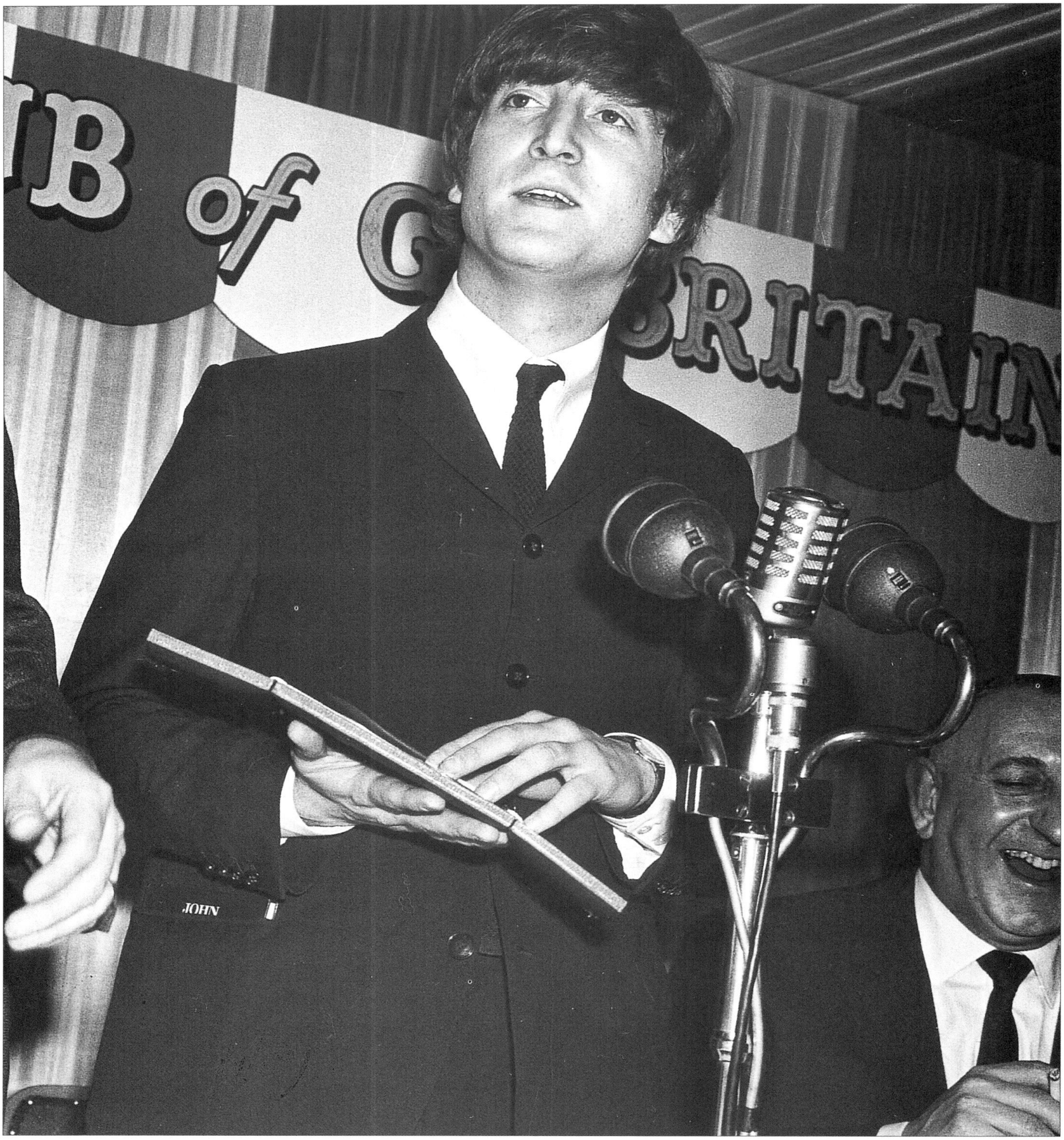

Ready, Steady, Go

John speaks at the acceptance of his award.

Opposite: John performing with The Beatles on *Ready, Steady, Go*, screened on March 20 prior to the broadcast of the Variety Club awards.

STEADY GO

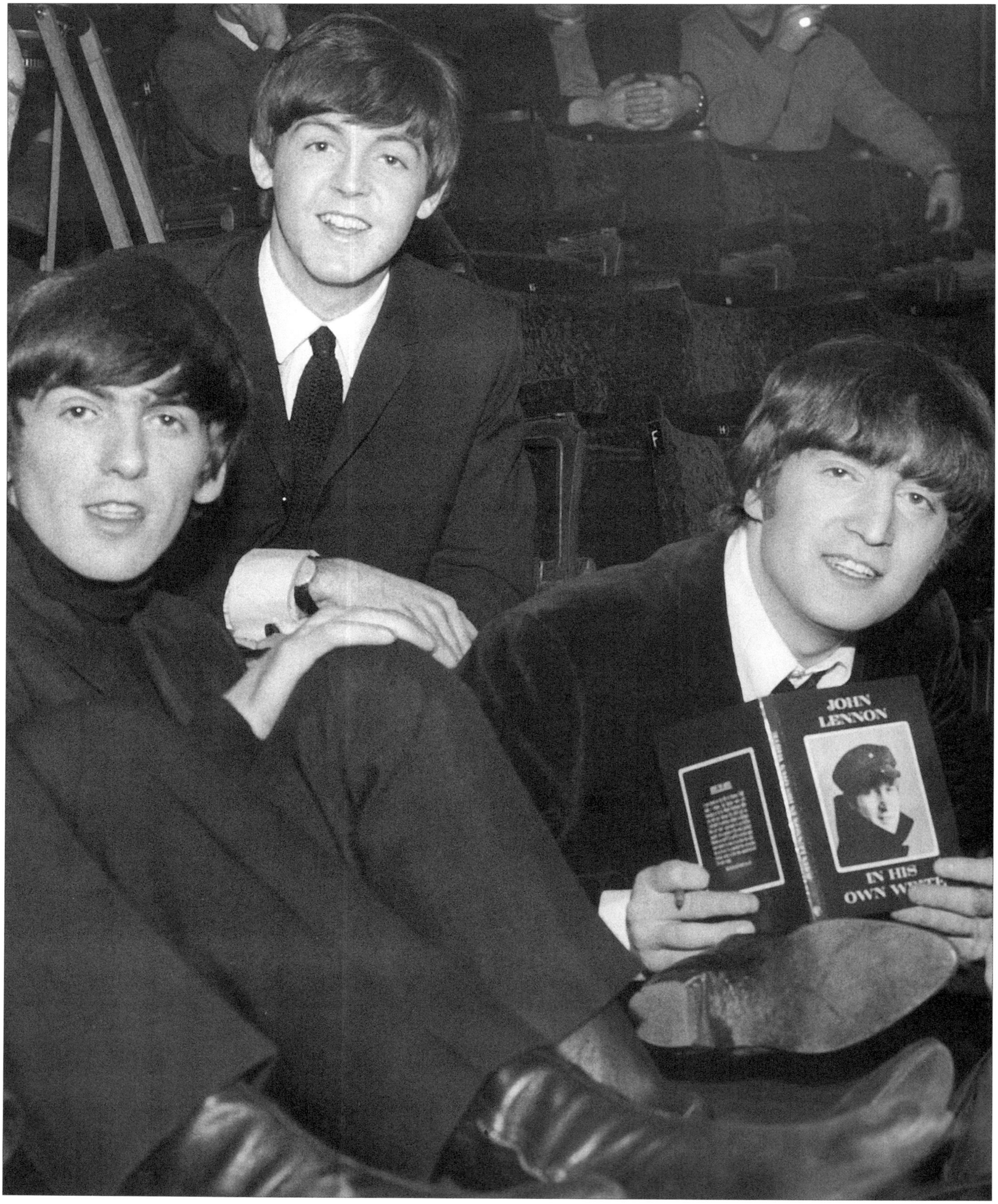
JOHN
LENNON
IN HIS
OWN WRITE

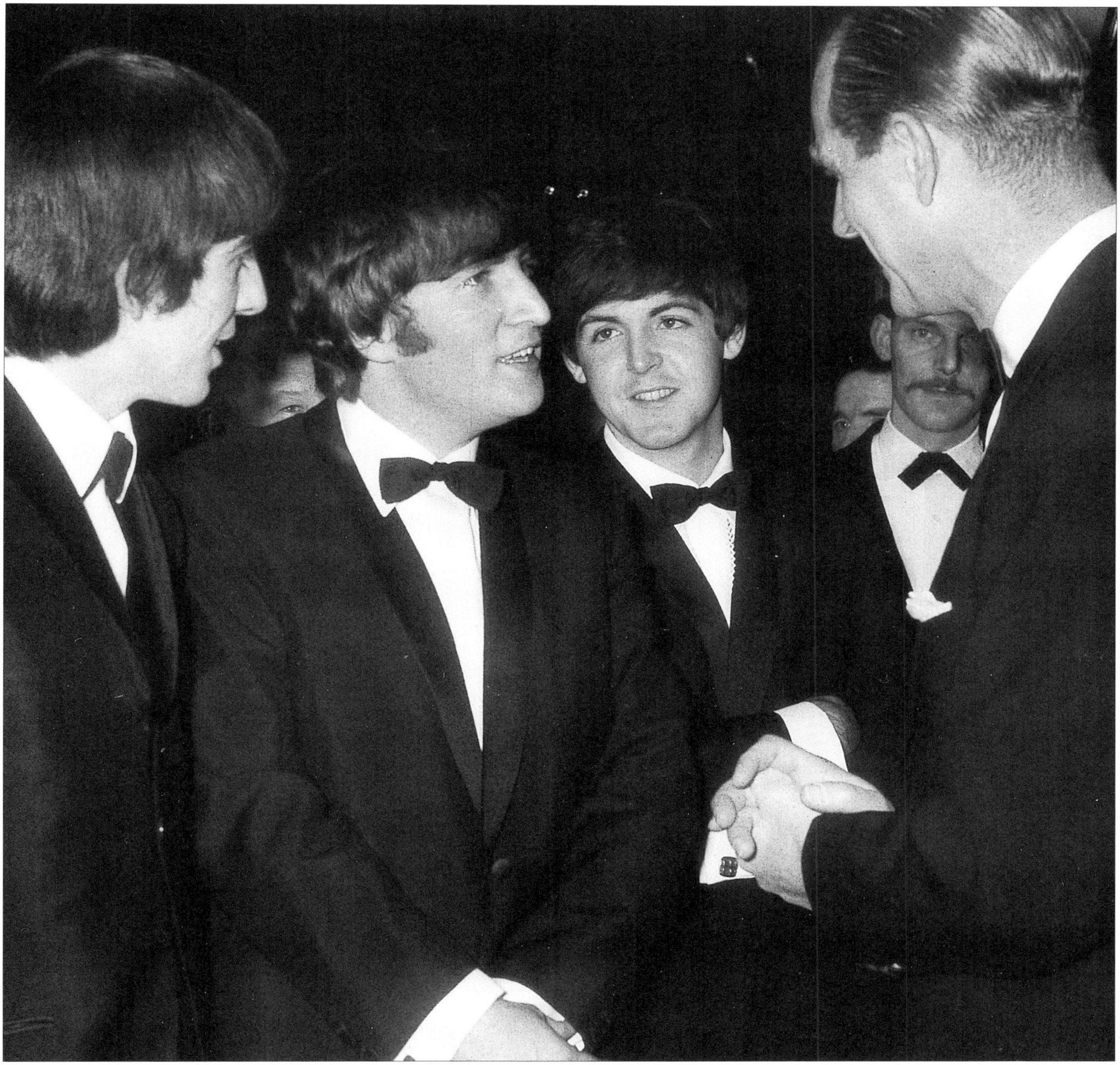

In His Own Write

Opposite: John pictured with his first book, *In His Own Write*, published on March 23, the same day as the Carl-Alan award ceremony. Also present amongst The Beatles is Walter Shenson, the United Artists producer who had negotiated a three-movie deal with Brian Epstein.

Above: The Beatles meet the Duke of Edinburgh, who is presenting the Carl-Alan awards, and John discusses literature with him. Despite their happy countenances, George and John in particular were beginning to become disenchanted with their courtship by 'the elite'. John was once quoted as saying, 'I'm sick of meeting people I don't want to meet. Boring lord mayors and all that... They keep sending in autograph books and we sign them only to find that they belong to officials, promoters, police, and all that lot.'

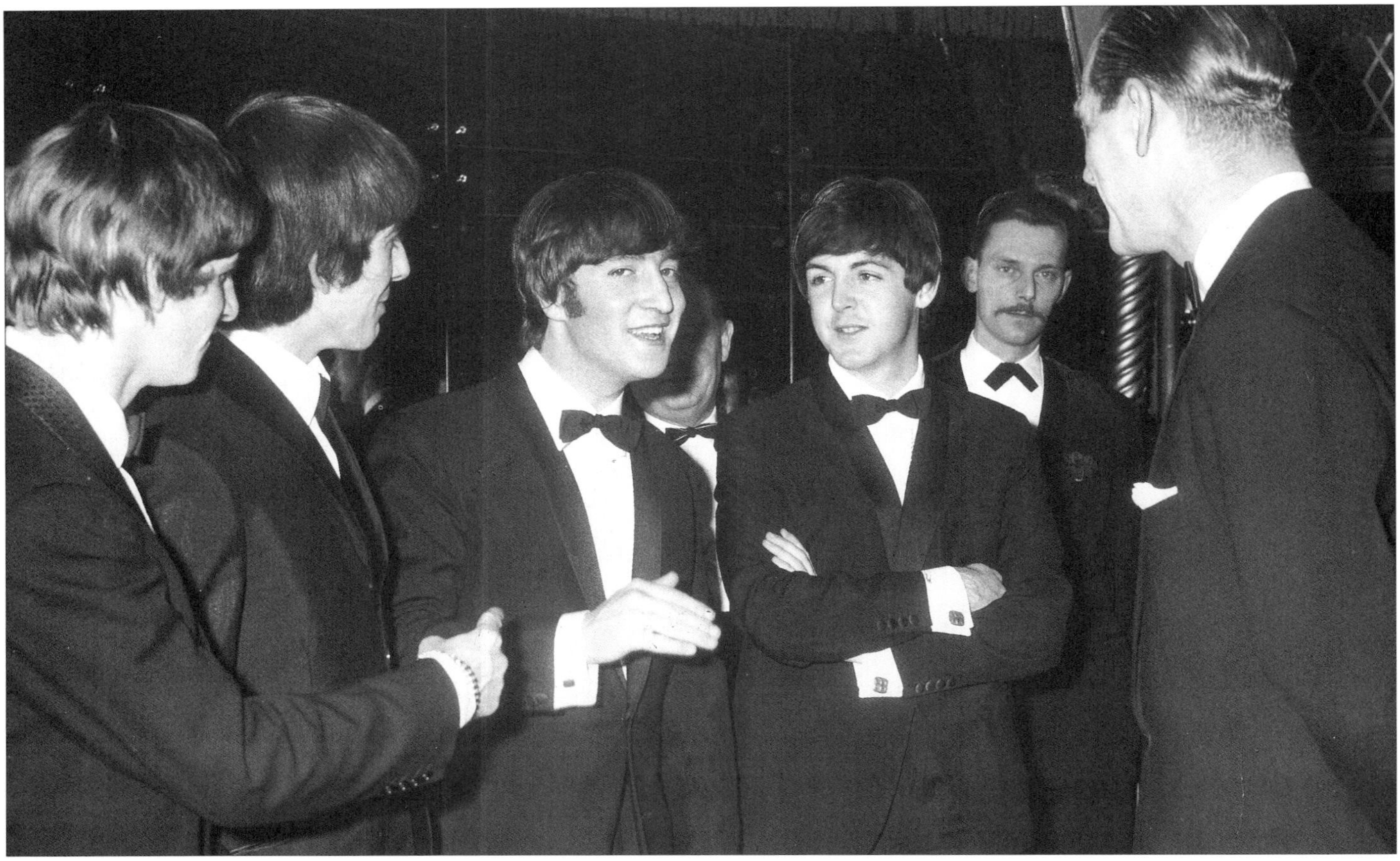

John's talent for word-play

In His Own Write was published to some acclaim, *The Times Literary Supplement* stating that it was 'worthy of the attention of anyone who fears for the impoverishment of the English language and the British imagination.' The book was really a continuation of *The Daily Howl*, a collection of doodles and nonsense verse, which John had produced whilst at Quarry Bank High School, and demonstrated his love of and talent for word-play.

Opposite and above: A month after the release of John's book, on April 23, a Foyle's literary luncheon was held in his honor. During the lunch, John shares a joke with entertainer Lionel Bart.

No speech from John

John with Cynthia at his Foyle's luncheon, held at the Dorchester Hotel, London. John disappointed some by failing to make the traditional guest-of-honor speech, saying only 'Thank you, you've got a lucky face.' *In His Own Write* was to prove a bestseller.

Now for book two

Right: John and Cynthia leaving The Dorchester. John was soon working on his second book, *A Spaniard in the Works.*

Below: Brian Epstein stands squarely behind his boys. He had always been aware of the value of television appearances in building the reputation and popularity of his stars. He had already negotiated for The Beatles to appear in their own TV special, *Around The Beatles.*

Opposite: A hard day's knight? The four Beatles rehearse for their forthcoming TV special.

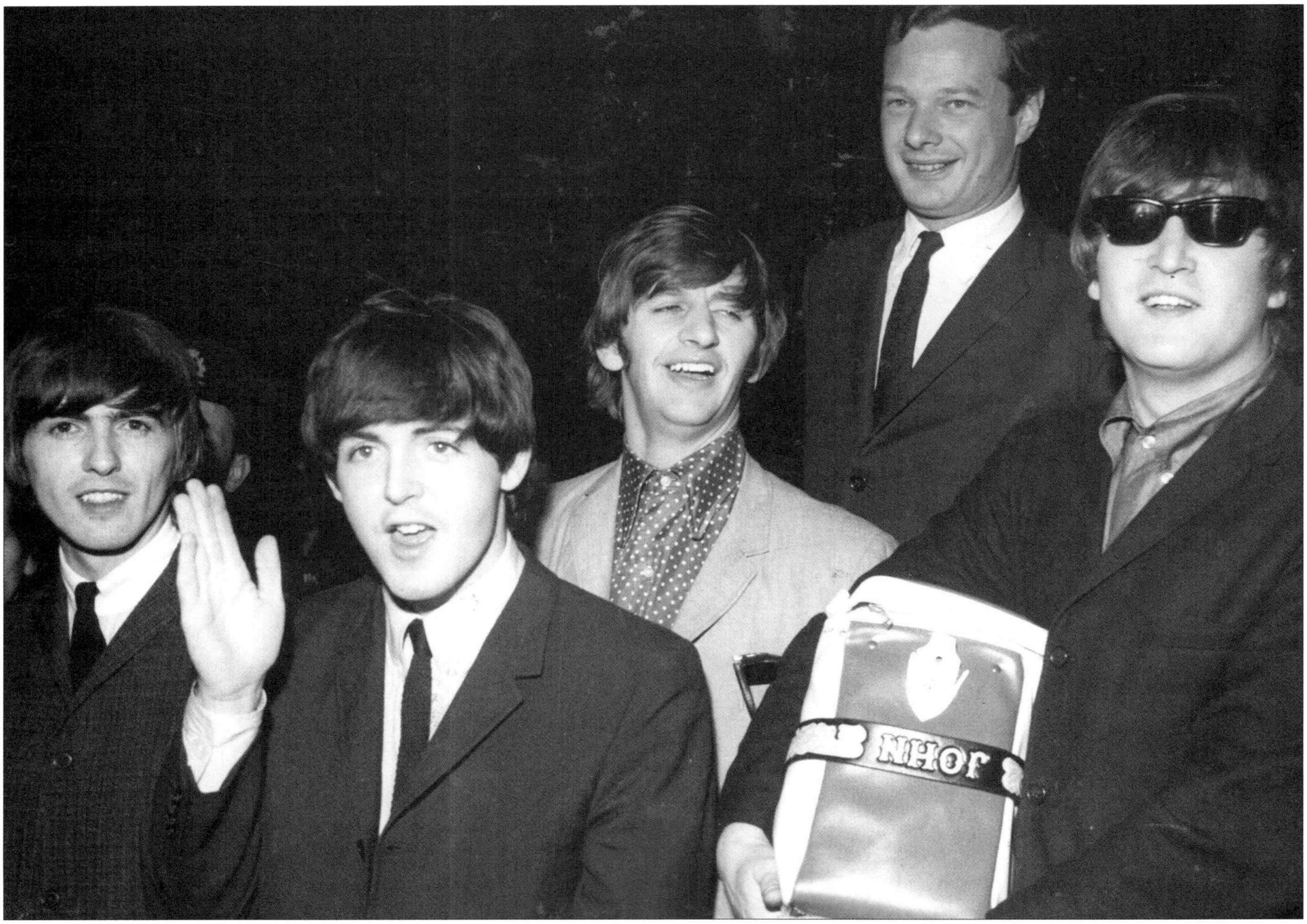

Spot The Difference…

The Beatles visit Madame Tussaud's for a preview of their wax effigies, before heading off to Scotland for two nights. Two years later, exhausted and disenchanted with performing live, John was to remark, '…we could send out four waxwork dummies of ourselves and that would satisfy the crowds.'

Opposite: John in a thoughtful mood.

Edinburgh

The Beatles, somewhat windswept, descend the stairs of their plane to a warm reception in Edinburgh. Their concerts in Scotland were so successful that they were invited to return later in the year. Just a few days before this trip, a new single, 'Love Me Do', had been released in the US - Beatles songs currently held the top five positions in America's Billboard chart.

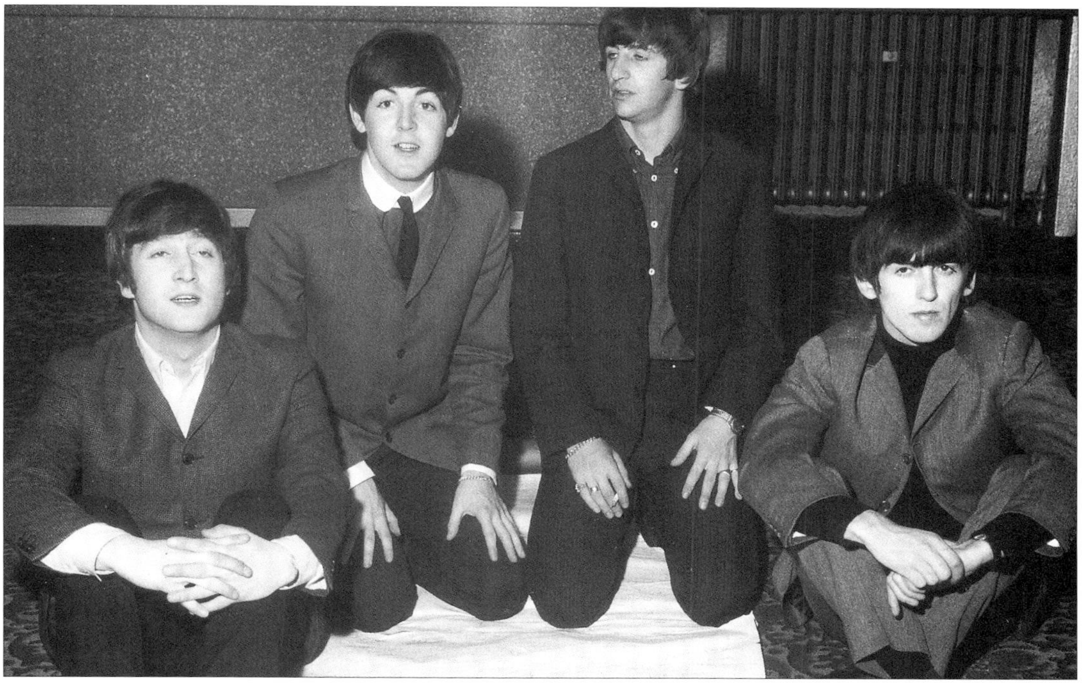

Genuine John Lennon

The Beatles meet a group of young fans in Edinburgh. In spite of his 'hard' image, and occasional dismay with the relentless touring and the excesses of Beatlemania, John certainly valued his genuine fans, especially the younger ones amongst them.

Opposite: John signs an autograph. He was very aware of his responsibilities to the fans and was conscientious if not enthusiastic about autograph-signing.

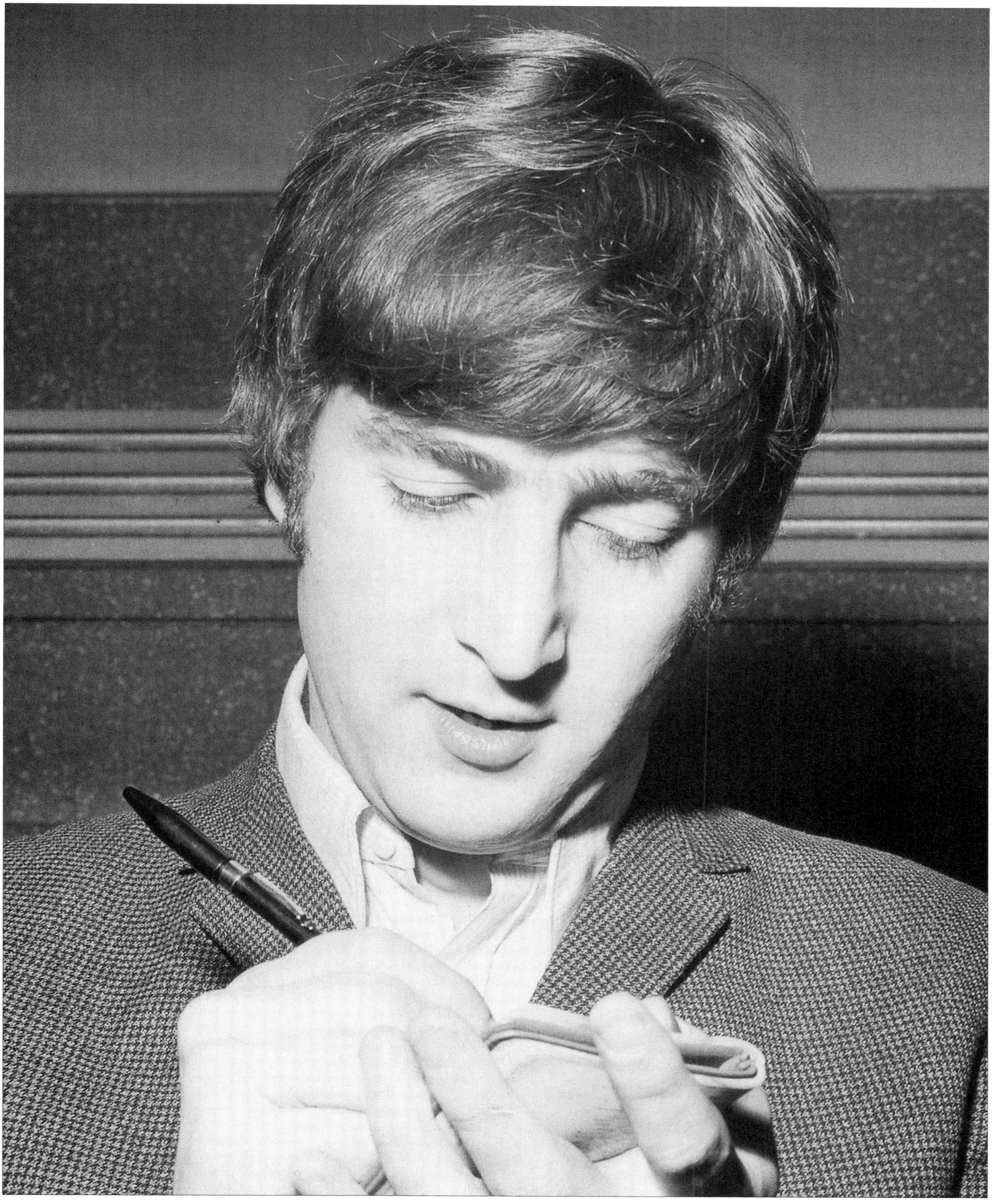

Feet on the ground

Although John had already become tired of the demands that fame and some of the more persistent fans made on his daily life, he enjoyed many of its benefits. By mid-1964, with record sales and song-writing royalties pouring in, he was a millionaire. Despite this, he still had his feet firmly on the ground in many respects. Although he tried many of the fads of the day, he also quickly gave them up if they didn't suit him.

Below and opposite: John at ease with younger members of the Beatles' fan club.

Relaxing with the Lord Provost

An informal meeting with the Lord Provost backstage in Edinburgh. John may have viewed authority figures with suspicion, but seems happy enough to sit and enjoy a pint with this particular dignitary. He even takes the opportunity to have a closer look at the chain of office.

Keeping it informal

Above: In general John and the others now refused to attend official functions, since they felt they were often regarded as some sort of freaks by the other guests. At one awful reception in Washington they had been pushed around by junior officials and ordered to sign autographs. Meeting the Provost backstage on an informal basis was a different matter.

Opposite: Waiting to go on stage, John and Paul take a break on a handy ice cream freezer.

Lyons

How do you spell it?

John scribbles down his name for another fan. He was not above writing nonsense instead of his signature - particularly if he believed the autograph book did not belong to a genuine fan.

Opposite: Lennon in thoughtful mode. He was prepared to do what needed to be done to be 'bigger than Elvis', but had already begun to realize that such a life was not genuinely fulfilling.

Below: The fans screamed so loudly at all the concerts that it was impossible for anyone to hear the music. John would often finish a song with a shouted obscenity - as a form of release from the tension - but the fans never heard it.

Which way now?

John was extremely short-sighted, but he refused to wear his glasses in public so he often had to rely on the others to get him where he needed to go. He sometimes wore contact lenses, but they were unreliable and often fell out at the wrong moment.

Opposite: One young fan collects the complete set. While in Edinburgh, John and the others were interviewed by BBC Scotland Radio for the Scottish Home Service program Scottish News, which was broadcast the same night.

On stage in Scotland

Opposite: The Beatles perform in Edinburgh. They also played two concerts in Glasgow the following night.

Below and following page: A last chance for photographs and another opportunity for a young fan to meet John and the boys before they leave Edinburgh for Glasgow. Thousands of Scottish fans had been unable to get tickets, but for the lucky few it was a night to remember.

Around The Beatles

John appears as Thisbe in a parody of Shakespeare's *A Midsummer Night's Dream* with the rest of the group, on the television show *Around The Beatles*. The program was broadcast in May 1964 and was testimony to the extent of their success in Britain by this time. However with so many guests, The Beatles only took part in two of the show's main items. On the other side of the Atlantic meanwhile, the group occupied the top five positions in the US singles charts, with a further seven records at various lower positions.

Well-earned rest

During their May break, The Beatles went on holiday separately - although later as the others also married or settled with steady girlfriends they often went together. Epstein's organization made sure that news of their presence rarely got out locally, so they were not disturbed when taking a well-earned rest. Here John and Cynthia arrive back at Luton Airport.

Ready To Take On The World...

The Beatles regroup on May 31 at the Prince of Wales Theatre, London, for a Press conference where they announce plans for their first world tour.

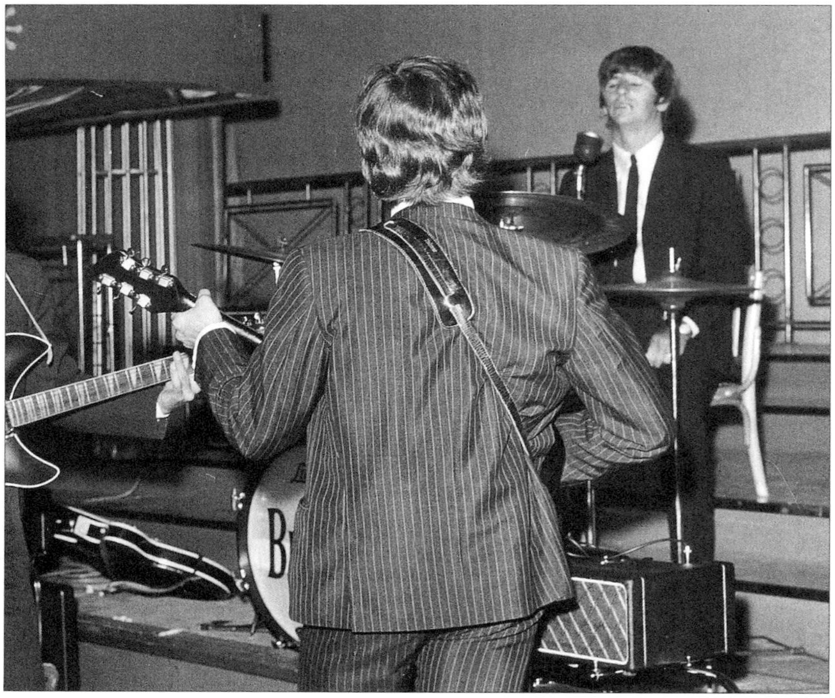

Scotch and Coke

A toast to the world tour at the Prince of Wales Theatre, with John looking a little distant.

Left: John with his back to camera warms up to play two shows at the Prince of Wales in advance of the tour, and also announce plans for five British dates at seaside venues.

Opposite: The Beatles enjoy another drink, this time in Leeds. As their fame and wealth increased during the 1960s, so too did John's drinking. This was perhaps an unavoidable part of being a 'swinging' socialite, and John could frequently be found emotionally arguing his points after a few too many of his favourite Scotch and Cokes.

DOUBLE DIAMOND
Vodka

The Shows Must Go On

On the eve of the world tour, with The Beatles preparing to fly to Denmark, Ringo is suddenly taken ill with tonsillitis. Session drummer Jimmy Nicol is quickly brought in as a replacement and is to perform with the group until Ringo rejoins them on June 14 in Melbourne, Australia.

Opposite: Jimmy with John and George at a quick rehearsal.

Below: Only hours after rehearsing six numbers at the EMI studios, Nicol boards a plane with The Beatles, bound for Europe.

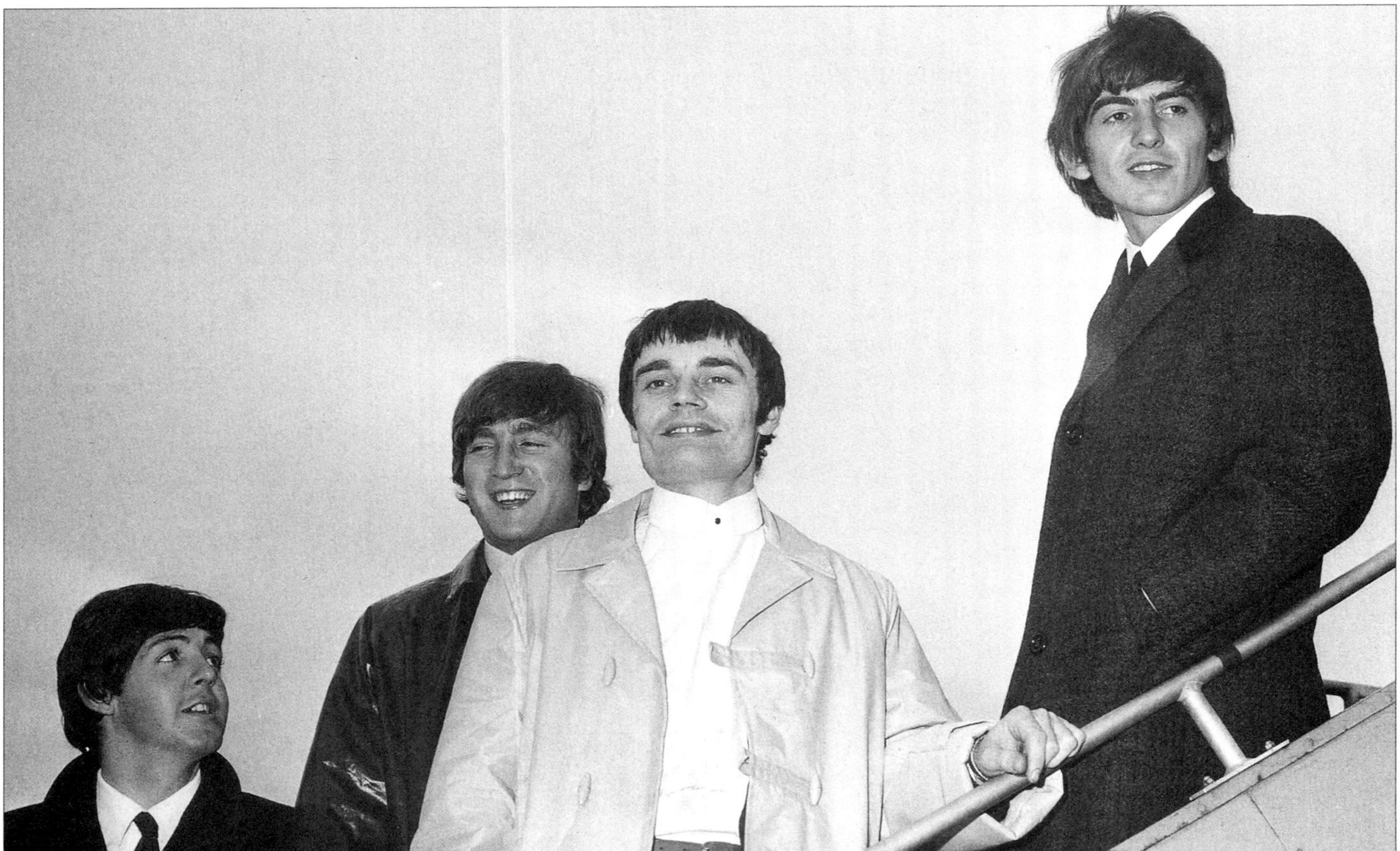

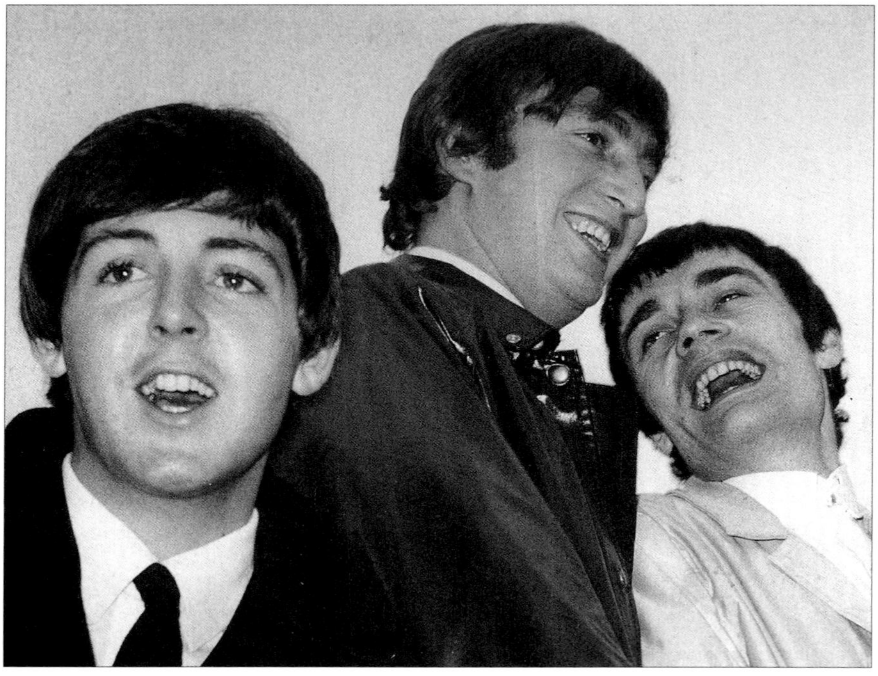

Down under and on top of the world

Although they were by now used to the hysteria that they generated wherever they went, nothing could have prepared The Beatles for the reception that they were to receive in Australia. Several attendance records were broken at their performances, but more surprisingly, the crowds that gathered at airports and outside their hotels were unlike anything that they had previously witnessed, even in the US. Hundreds of fans congregated in Darwin as their plane refueled, and an estimated 300,000 massed in the streets outside their hotel in Adelaide.

Left: John shares a joke with Jimmy Nicol.

Opposite: John and George look down at the crowds from a hotel balcony in Sydney.

John won't be quitting

Back from Australia on July 2. At a Press conference held upon their return, John was quick to deny rumors that he was going to quit the group - although the chaos of the tour had certainly taken its toll.

Opposite: Cynthia and John at London Airport as John arrives back from Australia.

Home Sweet Home

In mid-July, having returned from Europe, the Far East and Australasia, John and Cynthia set about looking for a new home. Up until now, John Cynthia and Julian had been living in a apartment in Kensington since moving down to London from Liverpool, though John was absent much of the time due to his touring commitments. Cynthia was finding it a struggle, with the apartment constantly besieged by fans, and so the Lennon family moved to a more exclusive address, spending £19,000 on a Tudor-style mansion, Kenwood, at St George's Hill in Weybridge, Surrey (opposite).

Julian Lennon

Above: Julian Lennon aged about one year.

Opposite: Meeting Princess Margaret at the London Pavilion. The Beatles' first movie, *A Hard Day's Night*, received its royal world charity première on July 6 1964 at the London Pavilion, forcing Piccadilly Circus to a standstill. It was to prove a resounding success, as was the accompanying album of the same name, and four days later The Beatles were given a civic reception at Liverpool Town Hall as the movie premièred in their hometown.

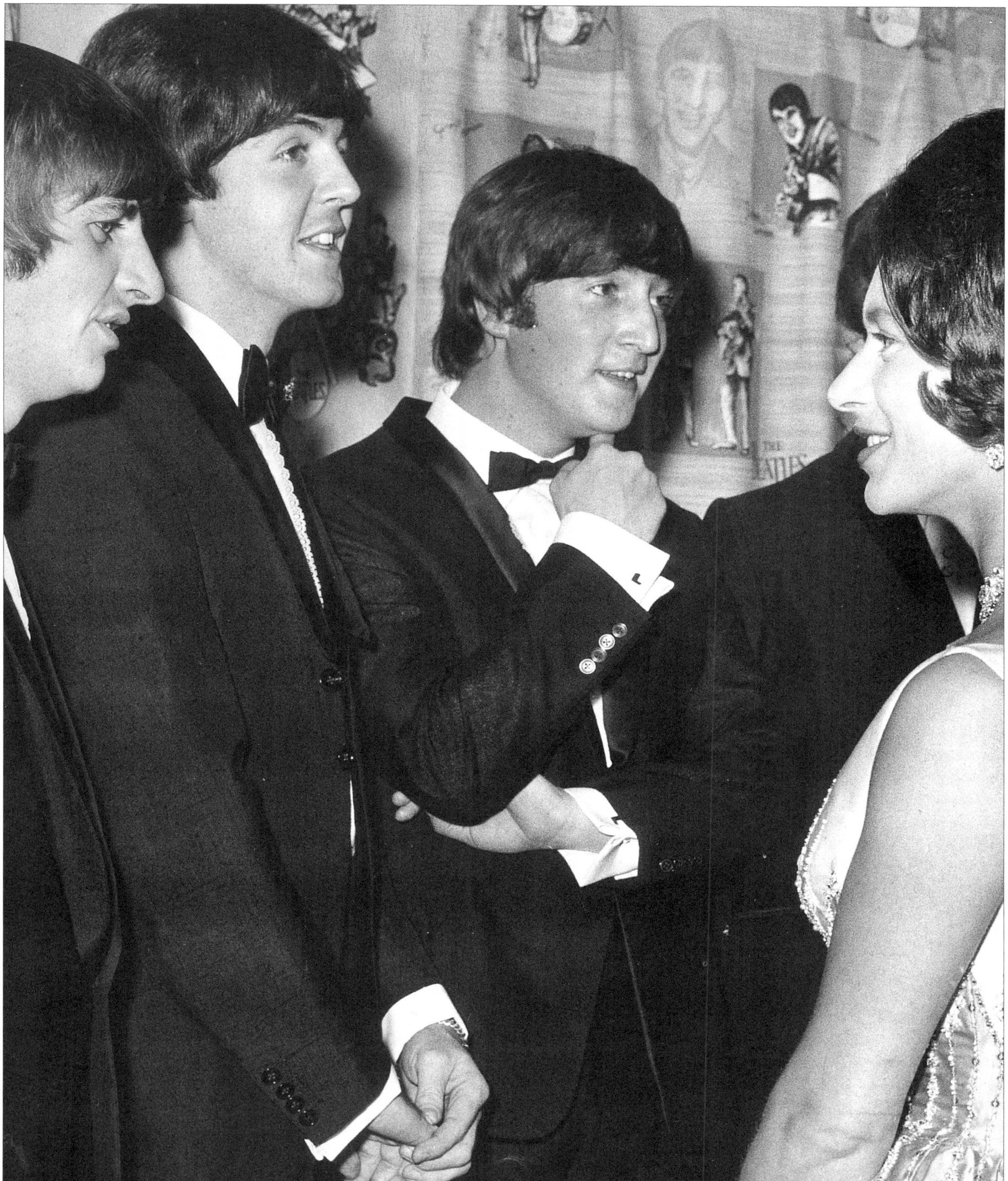

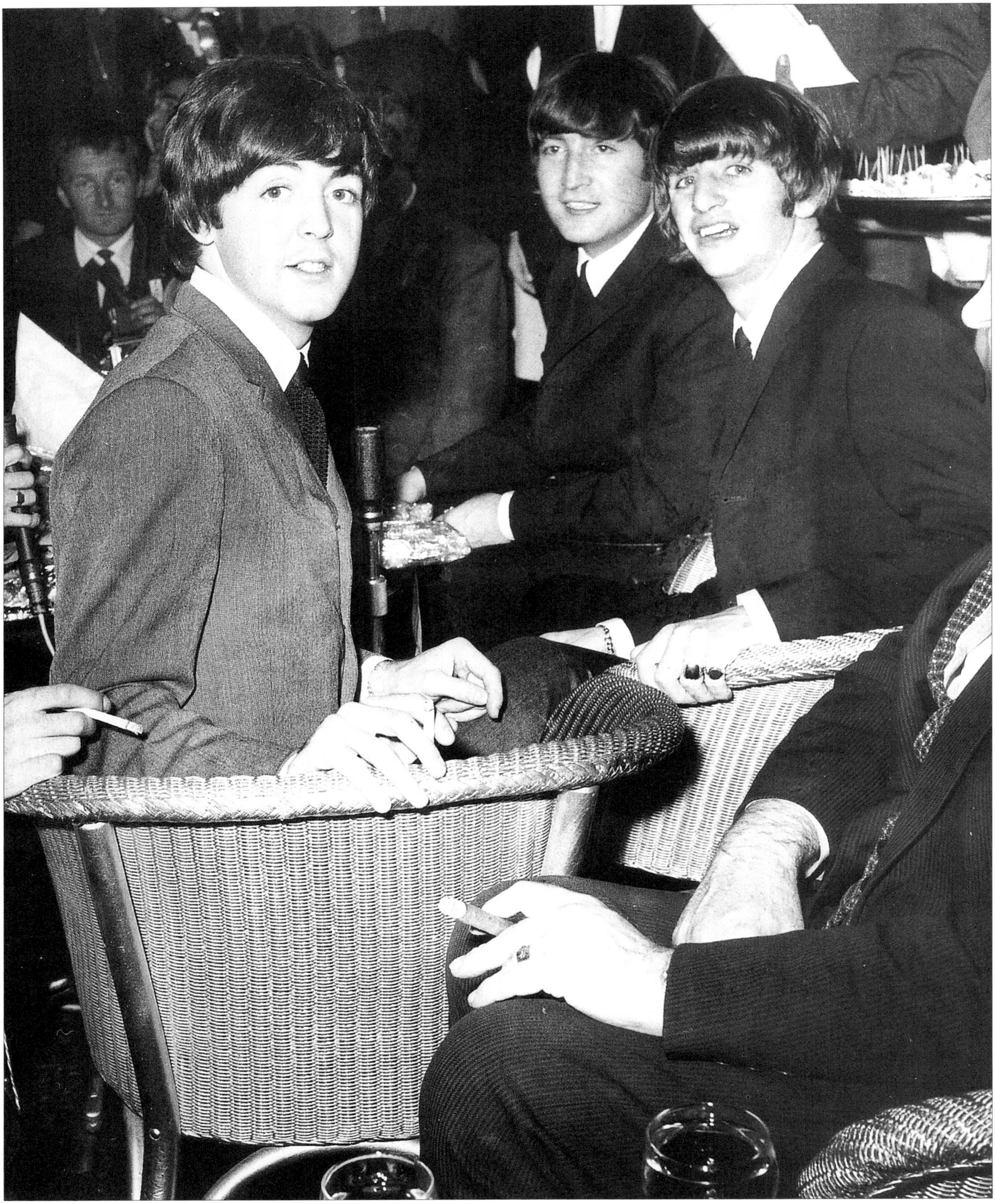

Honored in their home town

Opposite: The boys are honored in Liverpool at the Town Hall.

Above: Continuing their tour of coastal resorts The Beatles appear in Blackpool, performing live, and appearing in comedy sketches for the variety show *Blackpool Night Out*.

Blackpool Night Out

John in full swing in Blackpool. As well as performing some of their songs, they also appear in several comedy sketches.

Back In The USA

Opposite: On August 18 The Beatles returned to America for their first real US tour, encompassing thirty-two performances at twenty-four cities in just thirty-four days. Whilst such a schedule might have been commonplace in Britain, the vastness of the US ensured that they were almost incessantly traveling and Beatlemania was to prove more grueling than ever. The tour was obviously not without its rewards, however, and on September 17, The Beatles somewhat reluctantly gave up a day off to perform an unscheduled concert in Kansas for a record fee of $150,000. The fact that the fee exceeded even those for US artists was not lost on Brian Epstein, who was well aware of the publicity it would generate.

Above: Taking the applause in Blackpool.

Unstoppable

On arriving back from their US tour, The Beatles launch themselves into a series of British dates on the movie circuit, television appearances and studio recording sessions. Somehow, amongst the madness of touring they have managed to write enough material for a fourth album, *Beatles for Sale*, which is released in December 1964. The album is beginning to highlight differences between John's and Paul's writing styles, displaying John's increasingly autobiographical and introspective lyricism and showing the influence of Bob Dylan, whom John had met in August.

Above and opposite: Live in Dundee as The Beatles continue their British tour. As they travel round, two new EPs are released across the UK, *Extracts From The Film A Hard Day's Night* and *Extracts From The Album A Hard Day's Night*. It says a lot for the popularity of the group that such duplication was possible.

Another Beatles christmas show

For three weeks over the Christmas period The Beatles presented *Another Beatles Christmas Show* at London's Hammersmith Odeon. The show comprised both music and comedy and included guests such as the DJ Jimmy Savile. In one section the boys dressed up in Eskimo coats. Backstage, they recorded interviews and dedications for Radio Luxembourg, John mentioning ex-Quarry Men Pete Shotton and Nigel Whalley.

Above: At the end of an incredible year for John and The Beatles - it was only just over a year since they had last performed at Liverpool's Cavern Club - John filmed some scenes for the BBC's forthcoming *Not Only…But Also* comedy show. He was booked for the first program to read extracts from *In His Own Write.*

PAS CLAXONNER
MERCI

CHAPTER THREE

1965
Help me get my feet back on the ground

John had always been very fond of satire, as well as humor that played on words, and had grown up in Liverpool listening to radio programs such as *The Goon Show*. Early in 1965 he was delighted when he was asked to appear on Peter Cook and Dudley Moore's television programme, *Not Only... But Also*. The programme was broadcast on 9 January, and during the show John read some of his poetry. He was also a great fan of Peter Sellers' work and of Stanley Unwin, a comedian who turned the English language into total double-talk - and the influence of both these performers can sometimes be seen in John's own work.

In February John passed his driving test at the first attempt - which became front-page news in the British national Press. He had bought a Ferrari and a black Mini Cooper, and also owned several other autos, but he was never a good driver and many of his friends had cause to regret accepting the offer of a lift home. He also had a terrible sense of direction, so almost always got lost.

At the end of that month, The Beatles began work on their second movie, *Help!*, a comic strip adventure about the attempts of an obscure Middle-Eastern sect to recover a sacred sacrificial ring that a fan had sent to Ringo. This offered opportunities for location filming, so scenes in the Bahamas and Austria were written into the storyline. While in the Bahamas the group were filming in what they thought was a deserted army barracks, but John was horrified to discover that it was actually in use as a mental hospital. That evening, at a black-tie dinner with the Governor, he turned on the authorities and condemned them for allowing people to live in such conditions. The local Press were outraged, but John was unrepentant and was delighted when they left the Bahamas. All four Beatles had quickly become bored during the long hours filming and had turned to smoking pot to fill the time, so their concentration was not 100 per cent during the making of Help! Despite this the movie was completed in under three months, did very good business and was well received by the critics - although John himself never liked it much.

A Spaniard in the Works, John's second book, was published in June 1965. It was full of satire, send-ups of well-known newspaper columnists and irreverent features. In interviews at the time he said his writing was spontaneous and undisciplined, and that he hated anything to be cut, but often added things. Although he was an avid reader he had not read many of the accepted literary greats, so he denied that they had had any major influence on his work. Many of John's songs were inspired by newspaper articles - his Uncle George used to go through the paper with him when he was a young child, and had started to teach him to read using news headlines. This had instilled a lifelong interest in the news - and the habit of reading the paper - in his surrogate son.

John had not forgotten seeing Mimi constantly pestered by fans at Mendips the previous year. First he persuaded her to stay with him in Weybridge, then announced one morning that he was going to buy her a new house. When she was asked where she wanted to live, Mimi selected the first seaside town she could think of - and the two of them set off that morning to Bournemouth. After looking round several properties, Mimi decided she liked a bungalow overlooking Poole harbor and within a few hours John had bought it. In a fit of sentimentality, he wanted Mimi to keep Mendips, his childhood home, but she insisted it be sold - she wanted a clean break. After she moved, John often came down to see her, relaxing and drinking tea as he watched the boats sail past. Unfortunately Mimi did not totally escape the fans - the harbor cruises regularly came past her windows, and her house was always pointed out to the passengers.

Apart from filming and recording, John's life was still dominated by touring with The Beatles, with a European tour to France, Italy and Spain, another across America and finally a short tour round Britain. All four Beatles were now beginning to feel that this endless time spent on the road, along with the suffocating adulation from the fans, was becoming almost impossible to bear. During concerts John now quite regularly told the fans to 'Shaddup!' - or even worse - and even the others often stopped singing or playing for periods, since no one could have heard anyway. The music had suffered because of the impossibility of playing well under such conditions; they had once been proud of the fact that they were a tight group of accomplished musicians, but now hardly bothered to rehearse before a tour and often ended up playing abysmally at concerts. Who could blame them, when no one seemed to be interested in listening anyway?

During their American tour in August, John, Paul, George and Ringo finally met Elvis Presley for the first time. John in particular was a great fan of the American singer, and had copied the Elvis look and sound in the early days. The meeting was held at Elvis's Bel Air home, but it was not a great success. After some small talk they tried jamming together, then the four Beatles drifted away into the games room. A journalist instrumental in organizing the get-together said later that Elvis had been high on dope, and that the politics of the meeting had made everything too heavy.

1965 was also the year in which The Beatles received their MBEs. The announcement was received with disbelief - not only by the Press, but also by the boys themselves. Some of the battle-scarred previous recipients returned their awards in disgust, but John soon pointed out that they had received theirs for killing people, while The Beatles had been honored for entertaining - so he thought the four of them deserved the award more. In reality they had been honored more for their services to the British export industry than for playing music, but even so no pop artiste had received such an award before. Despite this, initially John wanted to turn the honour down as he felt it was all too Establishment, but in the end he was persuaded to accept it along with the others. After the presentation he gave his medal to Mimi, who for many years kept it on top of her television in Dorset.

One predictable result of John's fame was that his missing father had reappeared on the scene. Fred Lennon turned up on the doorstep in Weybridge one day in 1965, and Cynthia had no option but to invite him in to wait for John's return. John's deeply-held wish to hear about his childhood was at war with his distaste for an absentee father who had obviously come for a hand-out, and the meeting was uncomfortable and embarrassing. Fred was working as a washer-up at a hotel in nearby Hampton Court, but he soon began talking to the Press and by the end of the year had found himself a recording contract and released his own record - which did not do at all well.

Since they were fed up with touring, The Beatles had now begun to turn their attention to pleasing themselves, rather than the public. It was no longer possible to develop new songs on the road as they had in the old days, so they looked more to the recording studio, where they were working on a progressive complexity of sound. Producer George Martin had proved to be an intuitive interpreter of their work, and his classical-music training meant he was full of ideas that were new to them. Although Lennon-McCartney still appeared on all John and Paul's compositions, as agreed in the early days, it was usually apparent who had done most of the work. Paul's lyrics went for the heart, John's made you stop and think; generally whoever sang the leading vocal had written the song.

All four Beatles now had fairly settled personal lives. Cynthia and John were an established married couple, and Julian was two years old. Ringo had married Maureen at the beginning of the year and they also soon had a son, while Paul was living with Jane Asher and George with Pattie Boyd. Although this did not seem to have affected their popularity, during the height of Beatlemania the wives and girlfriends were quite often subjected to abuse and even attack from hysterical and jealous fans.

However, Beatlemania was finally beginning to show signs of running out of steam. In 1965, for the first time, some of the concert venues were not full to capacity and far fewer fans turned up at the airports to welcome the group or wave them a fond farewell. There were still plenty of fans, but perhaps they had come to realize that it was a waste of money to pay for seats at a concert where their heroes could be as much as 500 yards away and at which they could not hear a note of the music. However the music itself was still amazingly popular - the records sold as quickly as EMI could press them, and it was said that at any given moment in 1965, somewhere in the world a Beatles song would be playing on the radio.

Previous pages: John and Cynthia on a skiing holiday in St Moritz in January 1965.

Right: Whilst in there, John prepares for a bobsleigh ride with the British Olympic gold medallist Tony Nash.

The Lennons in St Moritz

Opposite: John takes a tumble on the slopes of St Moritz. However, in reality he had taken to skiing quickly and posed this shot for the cameras.

Above: John and Cynthia return from Switzerland. John had spent much of 1963 and 1964 touring, and whilst he cherished fatherhood, he often found it difficult to adjust to home-life after such long periods on the road, sometimes venting his frustrations on the people closest to him. Vacations such as this gave him and Cynthia a chance to enjoy themselves, and each other.

Left: The Beatles receive an enthusiastic send-off as they head to the Bahamas to begin two weeks of filming for *Help!*.

Drive My Car

Opposite: John congratulated at EMI by Paul, having passed his driving test in February 1965 at the age of twenty-four. John always loved cars, but preferred to be chauffeur-driven, admitting that he was never a very good driver.

Below: 1965 was to mirror '64 in many ways for The Beatles, including the making of another feature movie. *Help!* was to differ significantly from *A Hard Day's Night*, however. Where the latter had been a fictionalized account of The Beatles' experiences of Beatlemania, *Help!* was fantastical, and provided them with the opportunity of escaping London and visiting exotic locations. Flying out to co-star with The Beatles is actress and member of the comedy fringe Eleanor Bron.

John outrage at suffering

John had once joked to an interviewer that The Beatles' famous 'mop-top' hairstyles were the result of emerging from swimming baths in Liverpool. Here they climb from a pool in the Bahamas, fully clothed and soaked from head to toe.

Opposite: Relaxing with a smoke during a break from filming in the Bahamas. Despite the apparent luxury, John was outraged by certain situations that he encountered whilst filming there. After discovering people suffering in terrible conditions in a mental hospital, John raised the matter at a dinner held by the Governor of Nassau and was criticized by the local Press for doing so.

On location in Twickenham

The Beatles continued filming in Austria and in Britain at various locations. John and actress Eleanor Bron filmed a scene at Ailsa Avenue in Twickenham - John was to build a good friendship with Eleanor, and after filming, the pair could often be found deep in conversation over drinks.

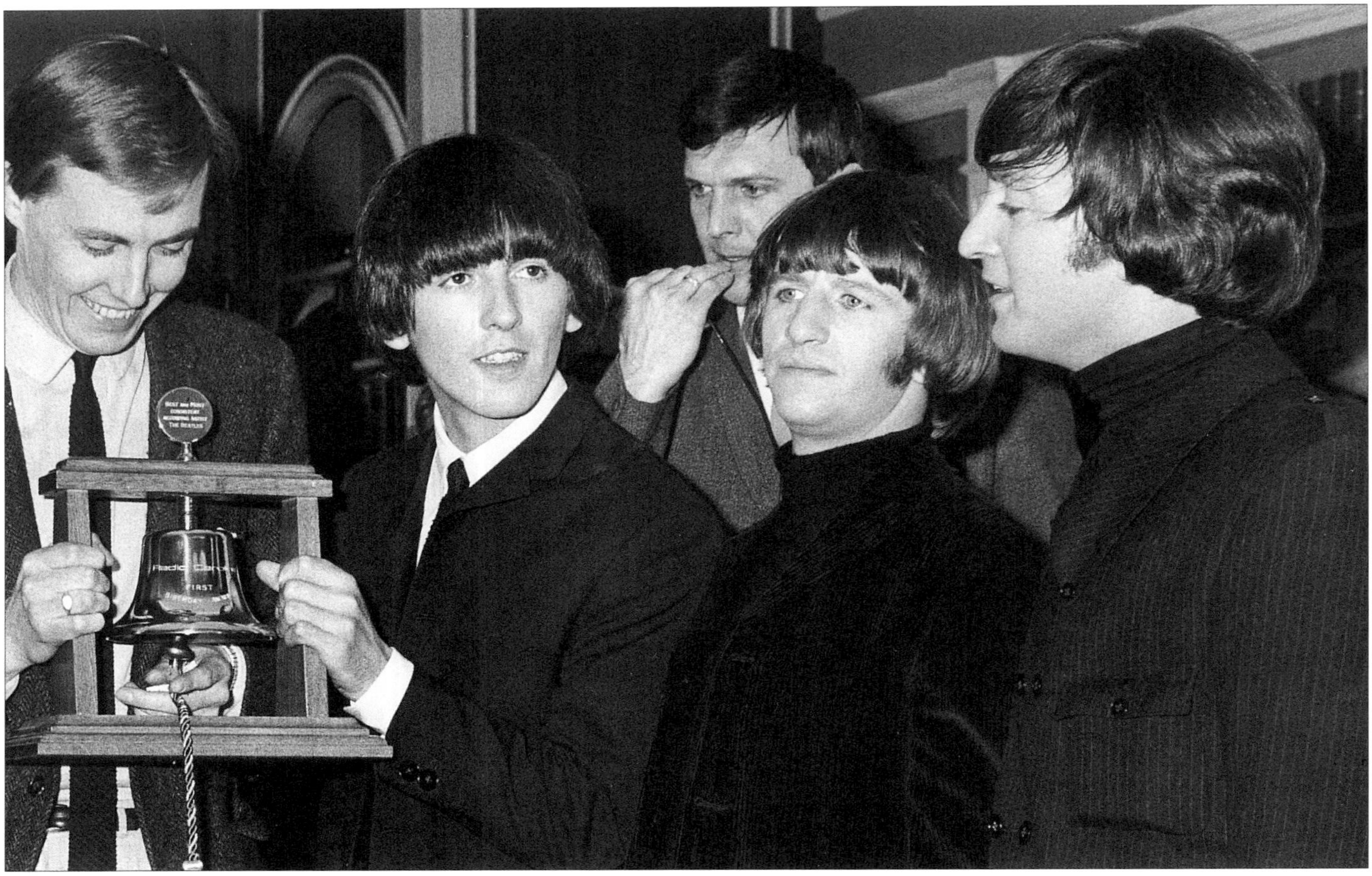

Celebrations

During the filming of *Help!* in Britain The Beatles were based at Twickenham Film Studios, London where they were to receive this award from Simon Dee, a DJ from the offshore pirate radio station Radio Caroline.

In June 1965 they also had a few other things to celebrate - firstly, at midnight on the eleventh, it was announced that all four of them were to be inducted as Members of the Order of the British Empire. They were the first pop group to be nominated for such an award, and there were some strong reactions. A week later Paul was to celebrate his 23rd birthday, and less than a week after that, John was to publish his second book, *A Spaniard in the Works.*

Right and opposite: John and George hold Paul aloft on his birthday.

Aunt Mimi's house

John arrives at the première of *Help!* at the London Pavilion with Cynthia.

Opposite below: After John discovered that his former home had become something of a shrine, with fans and Press constantly visiting the house, he persuaded his Aunt Mimi to stay with him at Kenwood. One day in August, having casually asked her where she would like to live, he took her down to Bournemouth and bought her this bungalow overlooking Poole Harbor.

Stadium Rock

The Beatles returned to the US in August, and this time hoped that with advance planning and extra security measures they might reduce some of the chaos of the previous two American tours. The tour was also only half the length of the last, but the venues were amongst the largest they ever played. Such a move was meant to fulfill even the highest ticket demands, and The Beatles performed in front of some vast crowds, but the stadiums were rarely filled to capacity.

The tour began with perhaps their most famous performance, to a crowd of 55,600 at Shea Stadium, New York, where they arrived by a combination of limousine, helicopter and armoured truck, before running the final yards from the players' tunnel to the stage and launching into 'Twist And Shout'. Regardless of the deafening screams which threatened to drown out the music, and which John found so frustrating, 'The Fab Four' were to give their all for this performance.

Welcome Home Lads

Back from America to be greeted once more by their fans. In Houston, Texas, only days before, The Beatles had been forced to abandon their plane as fans clambered all over it, but generally, fewer people were now turning up at airports to welcome them or see them off, and with The Beatles failing to sell out shows, it seemed that Beatlemania might at last be on the wane. John, like the others, was by now completely disillusioned with the live experience.

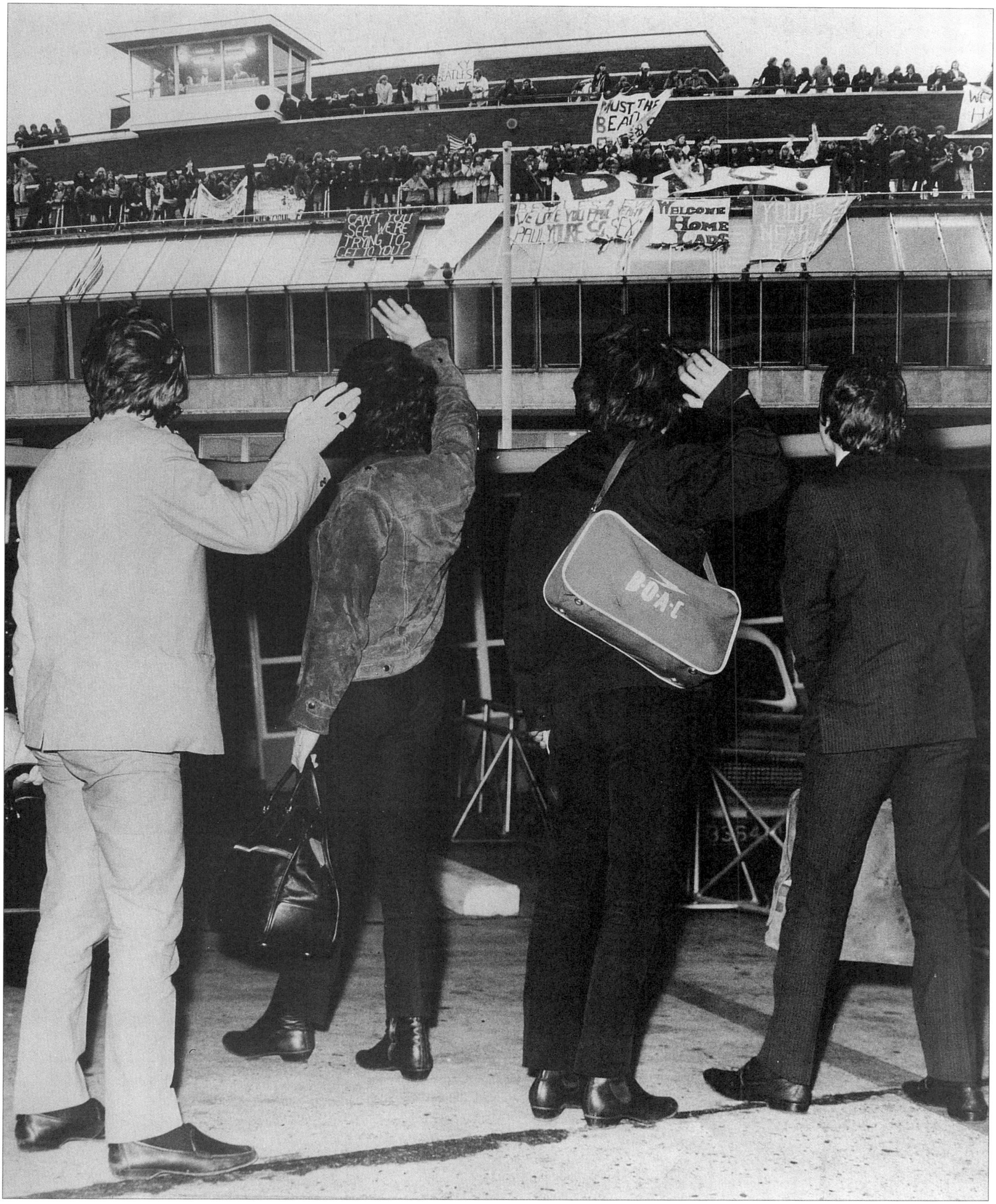
CAN'T YOU SEE WE'RE TRYING TO GET TO YOU?
WELCOME HOME LADS
B·O·A·C

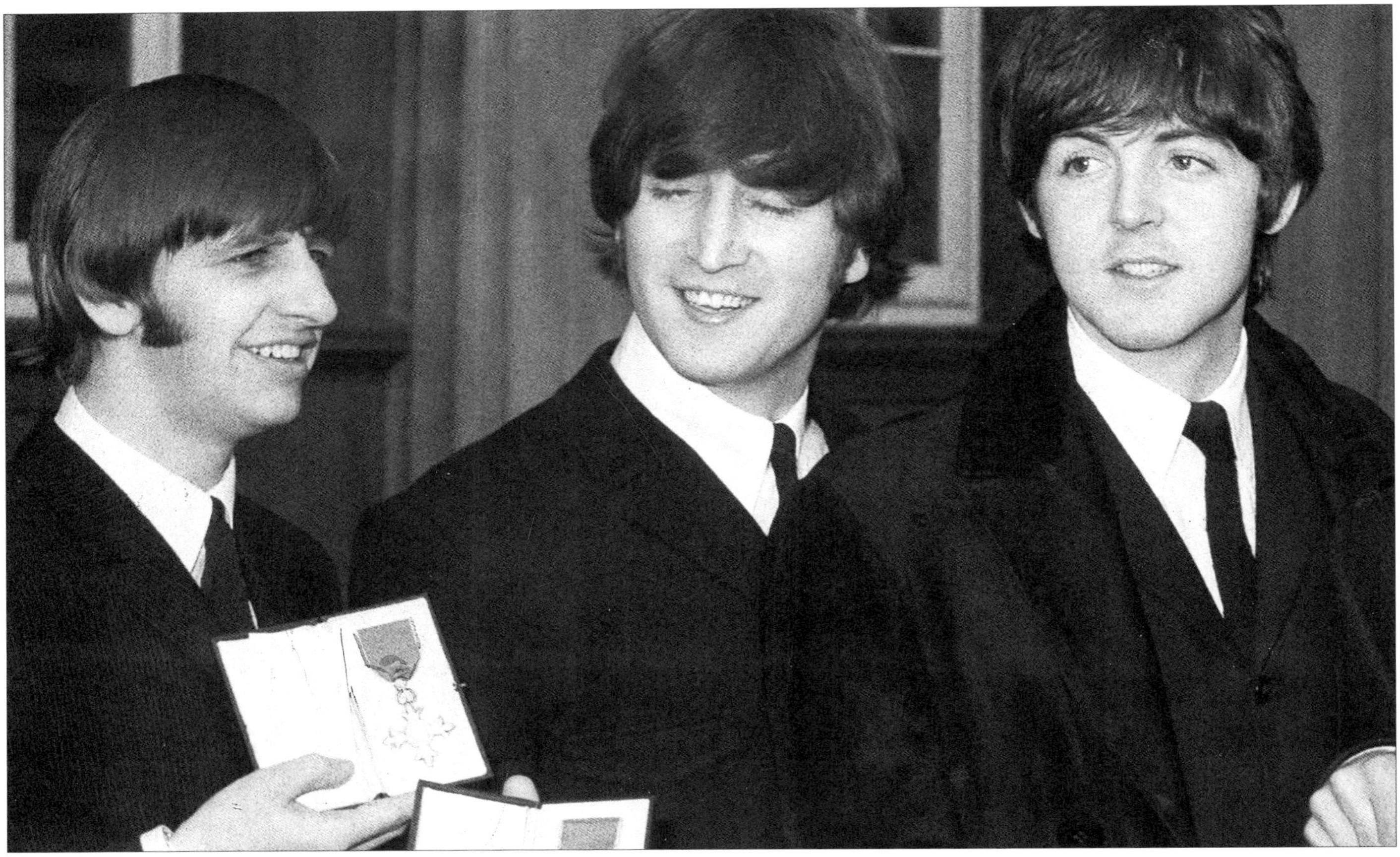

Members only

After some debate amongst the group as to whether to accept their MBEs, The Beatles attend Buckingham Palace on October 26, 1965 for their investiture. When military men started returning their medals in protest, John, who believed that such people had received their MBEs for killing, responded; 'We got ours for entertaining. On balance I'd say we deserved ours more.'

Opposite above: The Beatles leave Buckingham palace as the police hold back a crowd of around 4,000.

Left and opposite below: The Beatles show off their MBEs. Although protocol decreed that they were entitled to be accompanied by two guests each, they chose only Brian Epstein as their chaperone.

Rubber Soul

Unusually for pop stars *The Beatles* had always favored writing their own compositions over using material supplied for them. From the early days, John had written songs for other artists and had hopes of becoming more involved in production. As *The Beatles* began to exert more influence over their own collective destiny in 1965, learning to say no to certain demands made of them - such as television appearances and touring commitments - John was able to focus more on studio work and his musical craftsmanship. The result of this was the album *Rubber Soul*, which saw the group employing new studio techniques such as multi-tracking and the use of tape loops.

Rubber Soul was released in December of 1965, coinciding with the short British tour that was to prove their last on home soil.

Ludwig
THE
BEATLES

The Music Of Lennon And McCartney

At the end of the year a special ITV program, *The Music of Lennon & McCartney*, was broadcast nationwide. The boys prepare for the special with a sing-along at the piano and by enjoying the attention of a group of showgirls. The show featured several celebrity guests, who all performed Lennon/McCartney compositions.

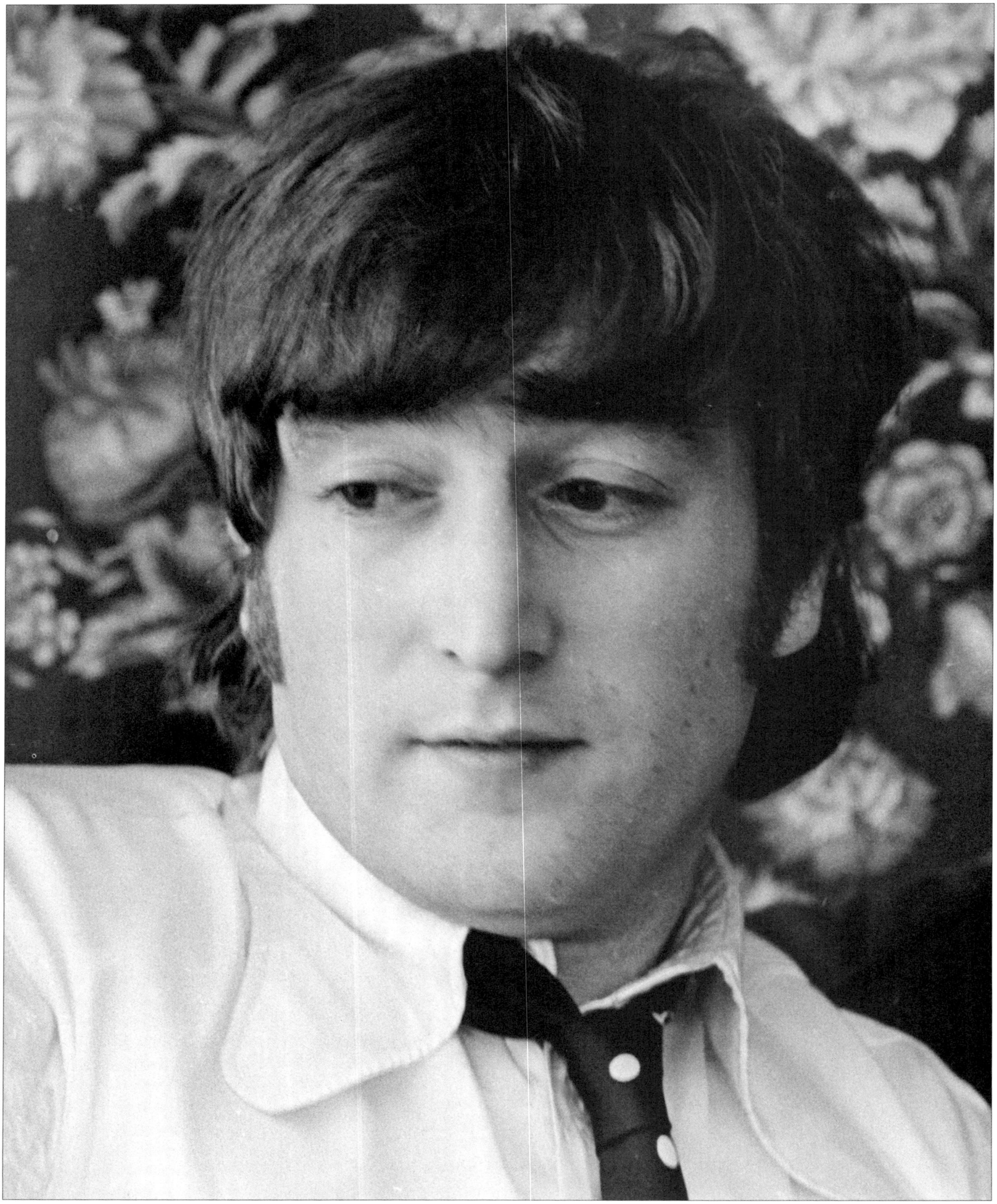

CHAPTER FOUR

1966
Try to see it my way

By now John wanted to stop touring, as did George. Their music was suffering because of the conditions they had to work under and the relentless attention of the fans was becoming more like terrorization than adoration - but another factor in their reluctance to continue was that they both hated flying. Both Paul and Ringo wanted to carry on; Paul was a showman who needed the audience's applause and Ringo just enjoyed being on the road. While they argued it out between themselves, the first few months of 1966 were spent in the recording studio, working on a whole host of new material.

In June, they set off on a short tour of Germany, Japan and the Philippines, which was a disaster from start to finish. In Hamburg, where they were welcomed back with open arms, John told the audience not to listen to The Beatles' music any more, because it was terrible now. The fans were deeply upset - although what he had really meant was that he thought they had lost the edge and excitement of the early Hamburg days.

In Japan, they had been booked into the Nippon Budokan, which was dedicated to traditional martial arts and had never before been used for anything else. Many Japanese considered it a sacred building so they were horrified that it was to be the venue for a pop concert; opposition was bitter and there were angry demonstrations and marches. Because of fears for their safety, The Beatles were confined to their hotel under armed guard. Of course John managed to slip away, but was promptly rounded up and returned, along with threats that all security would be withdrawn if they didn't all toe the line. At the concert itself, the fans were kept strictly in order, so they sat quietly and listened to the music. Unfortunately, since the band were expecting the usual mayhem in which no one could hear them, they had again not bothered to rehearse and it was immediately apparent that almost everything was mistimed or off-key. The fans probably did not care, but it brought home to John and the others just how far their levels of musicianship had slipped.

In Manila they all inadvertently missed a reception given by Imelda Marcos, which was taken by the locals as a snub to the President's wife. Ferdinand and Imelda Marcos were at the height of their power, and an apparent insult was not going to be taken lightly. Although there were no problems at the concerts, The Beatles were jeered as they left for the airport, security was withdrawn and they were jostled by thugs with guns. On their return to England, John told the waiting Press, 'When they started on us at the airport, I was petrified. I thought I was going to get hurt, so I headed for three nuns and two monks, thinking that if I was close to these people that might stop them.'

All this was as nothing against the storm that broke over their heads in America in August, due to remarks that John had made four months earlier in England. He had been interviewed for the Evening Standard newspaper, during the course of which he commented that Christianity was vanishing and that The Beatles were now more popular than Jesus. He apparently meant that Christianity was in such a state that groups such as The Beatles were better known than Jesus. His remarks were part of a much longer piece and passed without comment in Britain, but at the end of July the article was reprinted in the American magazine Datebook, under a syndication arrangement. This time they were taken out of context, and front-page headlines screamed that John had claimed that The Beatles were bigger than Jesus Christ. The American Bible Belt reacted with fury, with Beatles merchandise being ceremoniously burned and their music banned on an estimated thirty-five radio stations across several states. It all happened just days before the group was due to start an American tour. John was not bothered at first, and refused to back down, but it soon became evident that the anti-Beatles campaign was deadly serious and would be long-term unless something was done. At a quickly arranged Press conference in Chicago at the start of the tour, John attempted to explain his remarks - but journalists refused to be placated until he apologized. Under pressure he did so, although privately he was still convinced that he had not said anything that he needed to apologize for. He did have one unexpected ally, in the shape of the Bishop of Montreal, the Rt Rev. Kenneth Maguire, who said, 'I wouldn't be surprised if The Beatles actually were more popular than Jesus. In the only popularity poll in Jesus's time, he came out second best to Barabbas.'

The tour went ahead, but it became their last. The magic had gone and now perhaps it was actively dangerous. During the recent pandemonium they had all received death threats, and it was still possible that someone out there would refuse to accept the apology - when a firecracker exploded on stage in Memphis, each of them looked to see which one had been shot. When he returned to Britain, John told Cynthia he was pleased that the touring was over, but privately he did not know how to move forward. The Beatles had always been a touring band - now what would they do? He had achieved everything he had set out to do, and more, in just six years - and now he didn't know what he wanted next.

While he considered what to do about his future, he took his first solo movie role - the part of Private Gripweed in *How I Won the War*. At the beginning of September he flew to Celle, West Germany, to begin filming - but first he had to look the part. His Beatle locks were all shorn off in a regulation army haircut - and he acquired the famous wire-framed 'granny glasses'. Ironically, John had refused to wear similar spectacles when he was first diagnosed as short-sighted, but now they became his trademark - and they instantly became fashionable among style-conscious young people everywhere. John enjoyed the experience of working on *How I Won the War* but found the endless waiting around on set boring, while his attention span was too short to learn anything but the shortest lines. He could have been a fine actor - but he decided that it was not the life for him.

With his restless mind still looking for something to latch on to, John was introduced to LSD. It detached him from the mundane world, heightened his perceptions, and freed him from responsibility. One benefit to those around him was that his sharp tongue was less quick to lash out, and he became softer and less confrontational. He tried to persuade Cynthia to try LSD too, but after one bad trip she refused to touch it again. From then on they were traveling in different directions; it was the beginning of the end of their marriage.

Meanwhile, John had become more involved with the art world. It had been his first love before music, and he now he began to take an interest again and started to attend exhibitions and art-world parties. Cynthia was happy to stay at home, so John often went to these events alone. At the beginning of November he was invited to a private preview of *Unfinished Paintings and Objects,* by conceptual artist Yoko Ono. As he studied the exhibits, Yoko walked up to him and gave him a card, on which was printed the word 'Breathe'. One exhibit involved climbing a stepladder and hammering a nail into the wall. John asked if he could try it, but Yoko was reluctant, because the exhibition had not yet opened. Finally she said he could, if he paid five shillings. Quick as a flash, John replied, 'I'll give you an imaginary five shillings, and I'll hammer in an imaginary nail.' He thought the whole thing was 'nutty' - but it was fascinating as well. The two of them played the same mind-games and they could each feel the spark of attraction - even though both of them were still married to other people.

In November, John appeared again in Peter Cook and Dudley Moore's program, *Not Only... But Also.* This time he was in one of the sketches, playing the janitor of a 'members only' men's toilet. The program was broadcast on BBC television on 26 December, and it represented John's last solo acting performance.

During 1966, The Beatles released several singles, two EPs and two LPs, and at the end of the year they were recording another single, 'Strawberry Fields Forever'. However, that Christmas, for the first time in three years, there was no new Beatles album ready for release. In Britain, EMI compromised by collecting together some of the best songs and releasing *A Collection of Beatles Oldies.* Although they were no longer touring, The Beatles had by no means split up - but effectively they now only existed as a group in the recording studio.

Top Of The Pops

The Beatles rehearsing for their one and only appearance on BBC television's *Top of the Pops,* on June 16. They played their new single 'Paperback Writer' and its B-side 'Rain', which had been released just sixteen days earlier. 'Rain' had been written in the studio at John's home where he was experimenting with tape loops, so he incorporated some special effects into the music. The dreamy and distorted lyrics clearly reveal the influence of the drugs he was taking.

Previous pages: A pensive John after the US Press conference in Chicago, held so he could explain his remarks about Jesus.

JAL
JAPAN A

Hello to Hamburg

The Beatles embark upon their summer tour, taking in Japan and the Philippines, but their first stop is a nostalgic return to Hamburg. It is the first time they have been back since they became famous, and they are welcomed with open arms. However, John upsets the audience by telling them not to listen to the music, because it is terrible - although what he really meant was that he thought they had lost the edge and excitement of the early Hamburg days.

Last British concert

Left: John singing in the first live performance by The Beatles of 1966, at the NME Poll Winners Concert, at the Empire Pool, Wembley, in May. It was also to be their last ever concert in Britain. While this may have marked the end of a particular era, The Beatles were maturing, for not only were '*Rubber Soul*' and subsequent releases to achieve commercial success, they were also to receive the widespread acclaim of 'serious' musical publications.

Below: Protests in Japan over The Beatles playing at the Nippon Budokan Hall, which for many represented a sacred site, saw the strict marshaling of 10,000 spectators by 3,000 police deployed amongst the crowd. The band themselves were subject to similar treatment, being confined to their hotel rooms. When John managed to escape one morning, the police threatened to withdraw security entirely.

Opposite: John on stage.

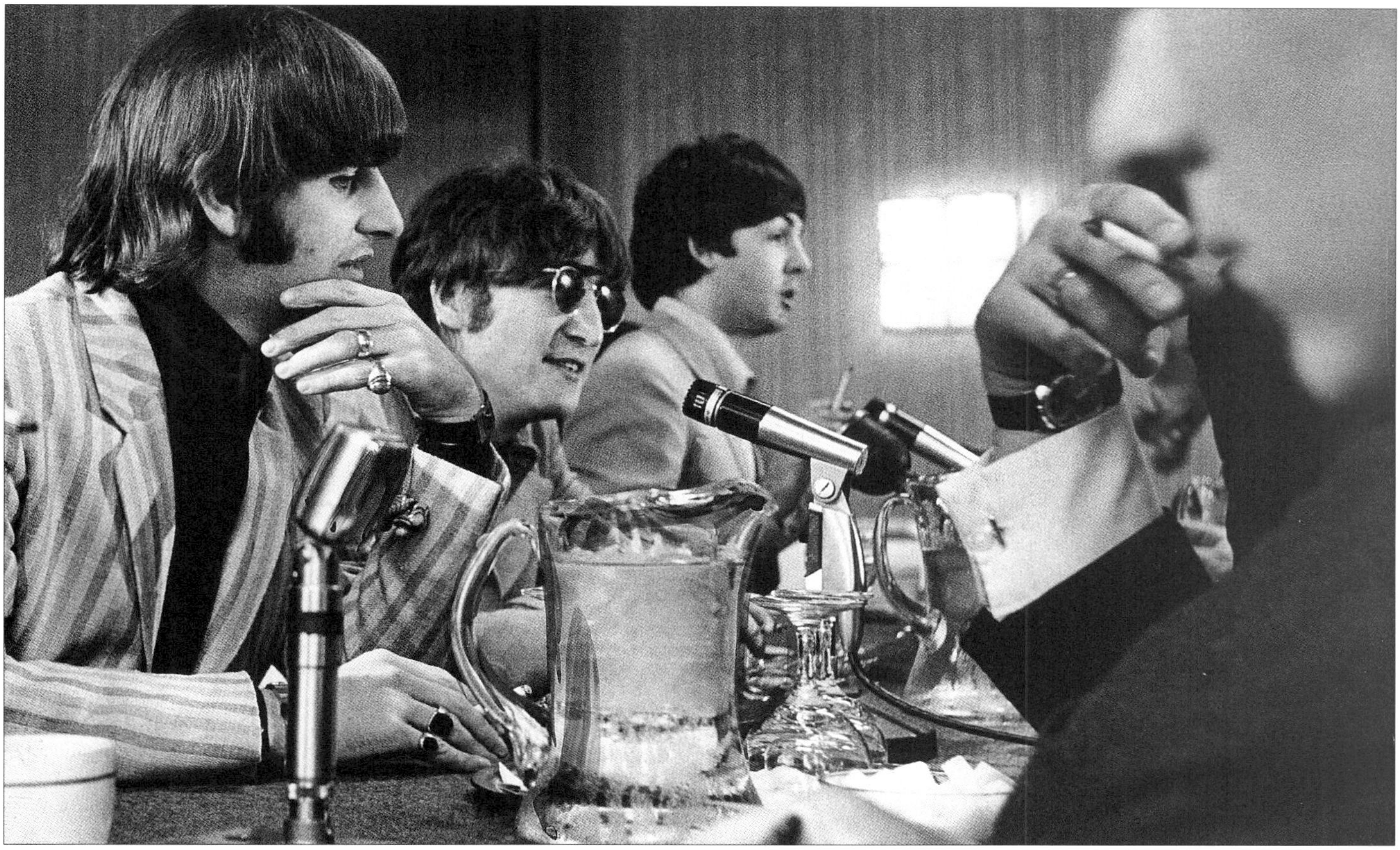

John: 'I was petrified'

If The Beatles had thought themselves subject to over-zealous treatment in Tokyo, nothing could have prepared them for the events that unfolded in the Philippines. On July 3 *The Manila Sunday Times* ran a story declaring that The Beatles were to personally visit the First Lady, Mrs Imelda Marcos, the following day. The Beatles had already ruled this out due to their tight schedule and thought nothing of it until an official came to collect them. Brian Epstein refused to wake the sleeping Beatles, and the newspapers ran the story the next day with the headline 'Imelda Stood Up'. Following this, things were made very difficult for The Beatles entourage, culminating in intimidation and physical attacks at Manila International Airport.

Above: On their return to England, John told the waiting Press, 'When they started on us at the airport, I was petrified. I thought I was going to get hurt, so I headed for three nuns and two monks, thinking that if I was close to these people that might stop them.'

Opposite: John practices the harmonica between shows.

The last American tour

Heading off to the US on August 11, 1966, The Beatles at least receive support from British fans.

Opposite: John in particular was fearful of what might lie in wait for him across the Atlantic. Back in March, in an interview published in *The Evening Standard*, John had remarked upon dwindling support for Christianity, commenting 'We're more popular than Jesus now'. The article hadn't caused a stir, but when it was reprinted in the US his remarks were taken out of context and provided more than enough ammunition for certain God-fearing Americans to organize public burnings of Beatles records and memorabilia. At a Press conference in Chicago, John attempts to explain what he had meant.

Left: The Beatles are shown around the new police station at London Airport before leaving for Boston.

John's apology

A Massachusetts State Trooper helps John through crowds of reporters as The Beatles catch a flight to Chicago from Boston.

Opposite: A weary-looking John Lennon collects his thoughts after the Press conference in Chicago. John had provided, with some bewilderment, the apology the Americans required, but that was not to stop Ku Klux Klan members protesting in Washington and various death-threats throughout the tour.

Safety fears

Although John was initially unwilling to apologize, feeling that he had only spoken the truth, he agreed to do so to protect the others. There was a very real fear of an assassination attempt during the tour - and when a firecracker was thrown onto the stage in Memphis, each of The Beatles looked to see which of the others had been shot.

The tour that followed could be considered a success, with all fifteen concerts packed to capacity, but something had changed for John. Now touring was not just a drag - the entire experience had turned sour after the events of the last few months.

Never again

A warm welcome in London, but unbeknown to the hordes of fans who greeted them upon landing, The Beatles would never again collectively take to the stage. When they left the arena in San Francisco on August 29 - having performed surrounded by six feet of wire mesh - it was for the last time. The touring simply had to stop, but no one knew if a group could survive without live performances; it was time to take stock. Finding themselves also between recording contracts, The Beatles were provided with an opportunity to rethink their strategy and to focus on individual projects.

Short back and sides… and those famous glasses

Of all The Beatles John had always appeared the most fiercely individual, but as he wound down from the experiences of Beatlemania he began to wonder what to do next. Dick Lester, who had directed both *A Hard Day's Night* and *Help!*, supplied the answer in the form of another movie.

Private Gripweed

Left: The part of Private Gripweed, in Lester's black comedy, *How I Won The War*, meant a haircut for John, and he was also to acquire his distinctive 'granny' glasses.

John was flattered to be asked to act in the movie, and the anti-war theme also appealed. Location filming was undertaken in Almeria, Spain, and at Celle in West Germany. After many years of having the company of the other three Beatles in almost everything he undertook, for the first time he was on his own.

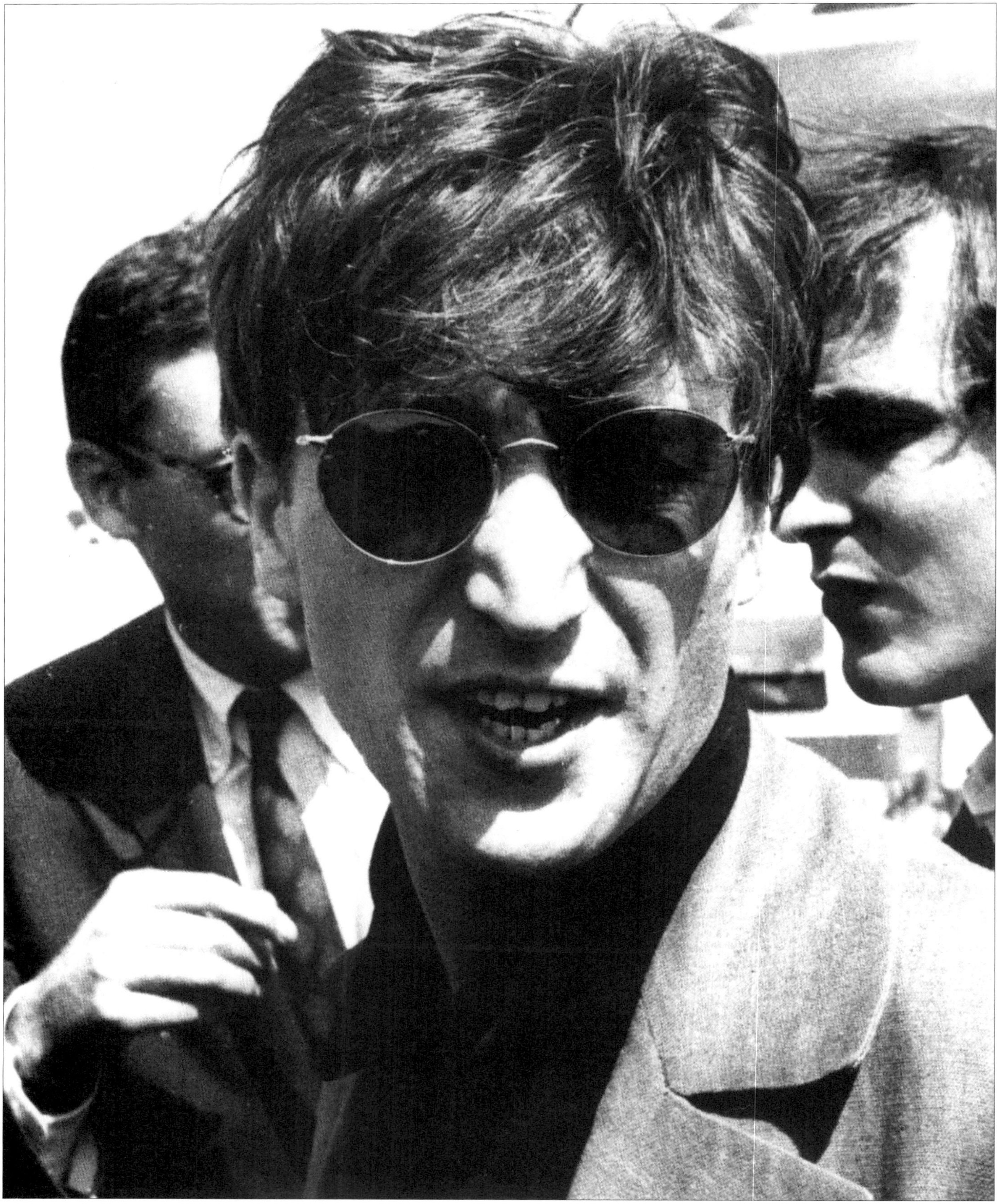

Enemy lines

Opposite: John arrives in Malaga, Spain, to continue filming.

On location in Spain, John cuts the hair of fellow actor Ronald Lacey. Although he enjoyed the company of some of the cast, the endless waiting around on movie sets bored him and he hated learning his lines, however short.

Strawberry Fields Forever

Above: John and Cynthia arrive back from Spain, where John has been filming in Madrid during November. Again he had to readjust to domestic life as he returned to Kenwood, but his responsibilities to Cynthia and Julian ensured that this would not take long - and besides John was quite a home-body at heart; he enjoyed reading books and the newspapers, and spending money on the house.

Opposite: John later in November arriving for the first recording session of new material at Abbey Road Studios, guitar in hand. The Beatles were to begin work on John's 'Strawberry Fields Forever', which referred to a place near his childhood home. The song featured him on lead vocal, and in terms of studio techniques, was to prove amongst the most complicated of all their recordings.

Yoko Ono

By the beginning of 1966 John was regularly using the hallucinogenic drug LSD, and becoming greatly interested in the burgeoning psychedelic scene and in avant-garde art. In November 1966, he met the Japanese conceptual artist Yoko Ono at the private view of her exhibition, *Unfinished Paintings and Objects*, staged at London's Indica gallery.

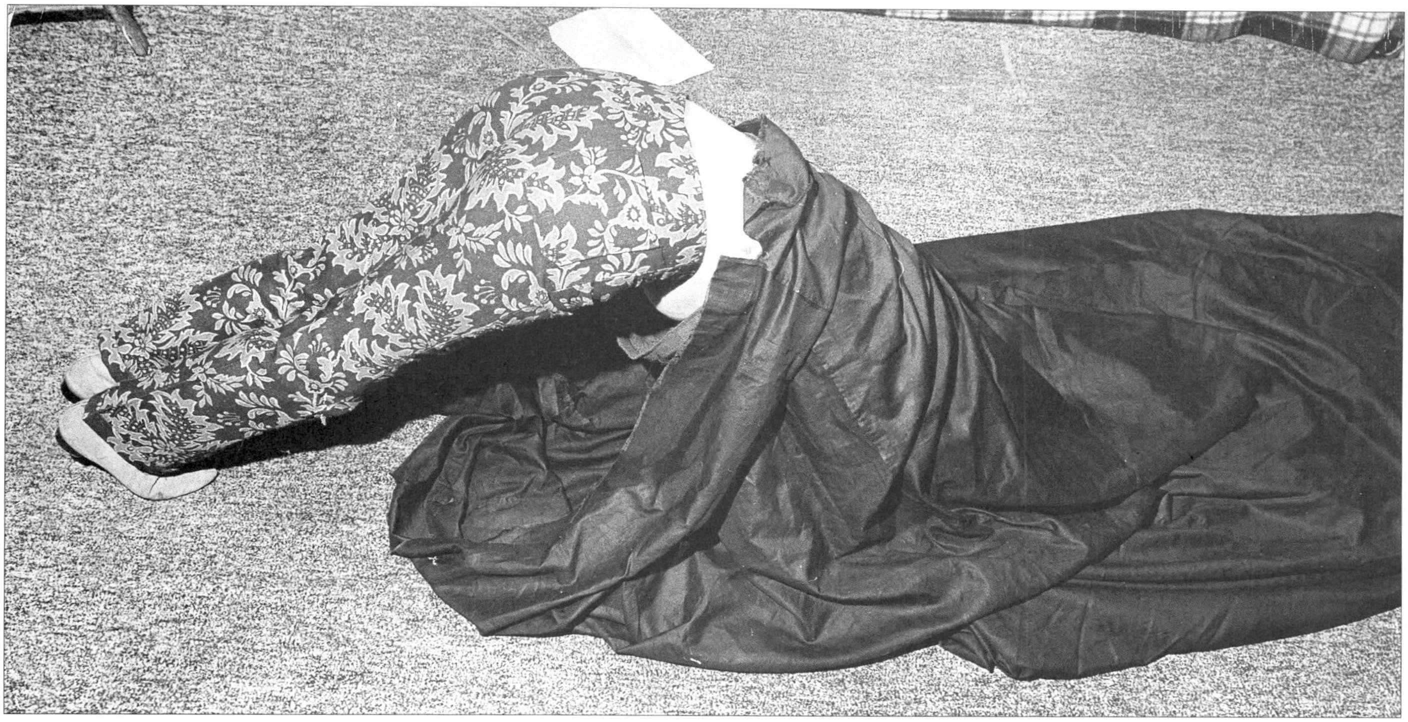

'Bagism'

Opposite and above: Yoko with various pieces from her exhibition, including a 'timeless clock' and a bag for hiding in. John and Yoko would use the bag extensively in later years, as together they developed the concept of 'Bagism'.

Right: John films a sequence for Peter Cook and Dudley Moore's *Not Only…But Also* Christmas show, playing the part of a doorman at an exclusive men's room.

Friends with Peter Cook

The exterior shots for *Not Only…But Also* were filmed in Broadwick Street in the West End of London. The show was broadcast on BBC television on December 26, and it represented John's last solo acting performance. During filming he had become particularly friendly with Peter Cook, since they shared a similar sense of humor.

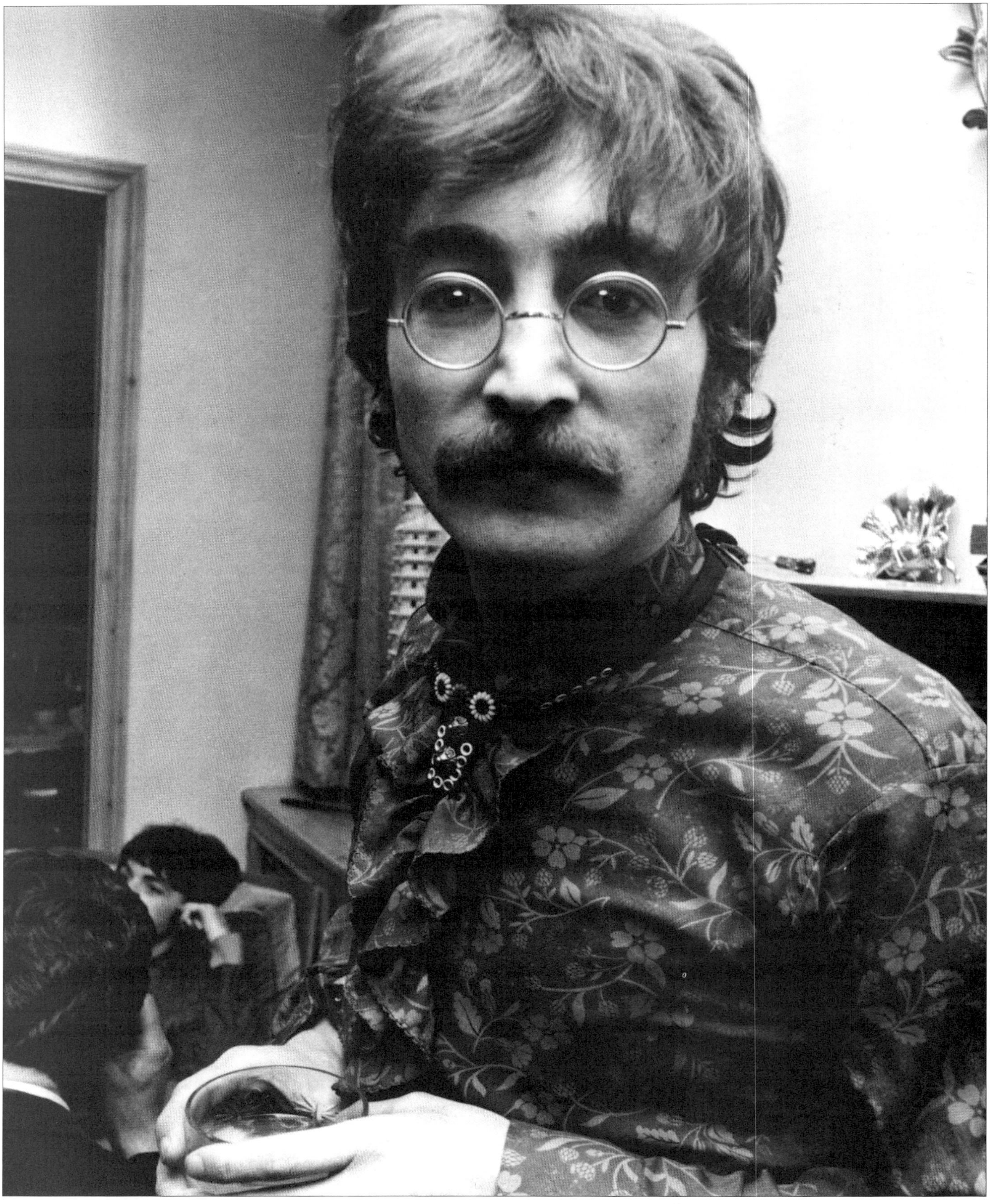

CHAPTER FIVE

1967
All you need is love

After their first meeting, Yoko sent John a copy of her book, *Grapefruit*, which was quickly followed by a stream of postcards simply printed with instructions such as, 'Dance', 'Watch All the Lights Until Dawn', and 'Hit a Wall with Your Head'. Although John thought they were weird, they caught his imagination and made him think. Cynthia had always accepted that John had affairs while he was away touring - and in fact early in 1967 he told her that he had often been unfaithful - but her attitude was that since he always came back, the odd fling was not significant in their relationship. Despite the fact that she was now married to a millionaire who was famous all round the world, essentially Cynthia had changed very little over the past six years. She was a wife and mother, and saw her role as providing stable roots for her husband, looking after their son and running their home. However, John had changed - and although there was nothing really wrong with his marriage, now he wanted something more. His relationship with Yoko took months to develop - but he was quickly intrigued by the tiny woman, with her long black hair and petite figure.

On the business front, John, Paul, George and Ringo had recently formed The Beatles & Co, a legal partnership to handle all their business affairs, which bound them together until 1977. Like John, the other three Beatles were also looking for new interests now they were no longer touring. Paul wrote music for a film and tried painting, George became interested in India and its religions and music, Ringo began to spend more time with his family. However, despite the different directions they were moving in, they still wanted to be together to make music and for some time they had been working in the recording studio in earnest to produce their next LP, *Sgt. Pepper's Lonely Hearts Club Band*. It proved to be a revolutionary step forward in their musical development and was instantly acclaimed by the critics, who believed it set exciting new standards for popular music. Since it was the period of flower-power, love and peace, *Sgt. Pepper* quickly became the sound track to Swinging London. The Lennon-McCartney partnership was now no longer really a partnership at all, as each was developing his skill in a very different way; John was becoming introspective and writing psychedelic and disorientating lyrics, while Paul's songs were much more bright, breezy and commercial.

The Beatles' 'loveable moptop' image took rather a battering in May 1967, when 'A Day in the Life' from Sgt. Pepper became the first Beatles song to be banned by the BBC, because of its supposed drug references. The powers-that-be had taken exception to the words, 'went upstairs and had a smoke'. Soon afterwards, Paul admitted on television that he had taken LSD and the following month John and the others signed a petition published in *The Times*, calling for the legalization of marijuana. The Press were quick to condemn them, but to young people everywhere it just added to The Beatles' street-cred.

However, despite all this The Beatles still held an unassailable position in popular culture, and they were chosen to compose a song for the *Our World* television show, which was to be broadcast on a global link-up across the world in June. The brief was for something simple, suitable for varying cultures, and John came up with *All You Need is Love*. Despite the importance of the occasion, the composer played it cool and chewed gum as he sang before 400 million people across five continents. The song went on to top the charts and became the anthem for the hippie generation. The broadcast was significant for another reason as well: it was the last time The Beatles appeared together live on television.

That summer, John decided that it might be a great idea if The Beatles bought themselves a Greek island, where they could all go to escape the endless intrusions on their privacy. He complained that fans still seemed to think that his home was some sort of holiday park, and constantly camped outside with thermos flasks of tea and sandwiches hoping to get a glimpse of him. He and the others went over to Greece to begin negotiating, but they all pulled out of the deal when it became apparent that Greek officials were planning to use it for publicity and propaganda purposes.

John, Paul and George were still looking for some sort of meaning to life, and in August they were all introduced to the Maharishi Mahesh Yogi during his visit to London, by George's wife, Pattie. All four Beatles threw themselves behind his movement and they soon decided to follow him to Bangor in Wales to study transcendental meditation. Cynthia managed to miss the train taking them all and arrived later, to be berated by John to the point of tears for always being late. It underlined the growing split in their marriage.

While they were in Wales, news came of Brian Epstein's death from an accidental overdose of sleeping tablets. Despite their rather laid-back public response to the news, they were all devastated. John, in particular, felt that without a manager to lead and organize them they were finished. At an emergency meeting held at Paul's house a few days after Brian's death, they discussed their future. Paul took charge and suggested that they should start work on a project that had been postponed for some time: the filming of the *Magical Mystery Tour*.

The basis of this project was that they should all pile into a bus with a film crew and various other passengers, and just drive round southern England filming the adventures they were sure to have. There was no firm script, no experienced director and no one had any idea what they were doing. John went along with the concept, although he resented Paul assuming leadership of The Beatles. The resulting ten hours of film took eleven weeks to edit down into the final one-hour version, and the entire project cost in the region of £75,000. When it was shown on BBC television at Christmas and was savagely criticized, John dubbed it 'the most expensive home movie ever'.

Soon after they returned from filming *Magical Mystery Tour* in the West Country, an exhibition of Yoko's work opened at London's Lisson Art Gallery. It was called *Half-Wind Show*, and it consisted of several everyday objects - a chair, washbasin, pillow - all cut in half. The show was subtitled *Yoko plus Me*: the 'Me' was John, who had sponsored it, but insisted on remaining anonymous and did not attend. He was beginning to quietly move away from his rather conventional home life in stockbroker Surrey - the signs were already becoming apparent for anyone who cared to look. He was increasingly involved with the art world and his drug-taking was becoming extremely heavy, despite Cynthia's disapproval. The other homes around theirs were boringly staid, but their garden now sported a traditional wooden gypsy caravan, which was painted in psychedelic colors, and his sober black Rolls-Royce was given a brilliantly-colored paint job to match. John had always had an individualistic streak, but his increasing involvement with Yoko was now giving him the confidence and impetus to break out of the pattern he had been forced into by circumstances, and do his own thing.

Meanwhile The Beatles as a group had moved on to other things. They now saw themselves as businessmen, building their own empire in which they would be in total control The first manifestation of this, the Apple Boutique, opened on Baker Street at the beginning of December 1967. The Apple organization was not intended solely to handle their own business interests; both Paul and George hoped that it would also operate philanthropically to foster new talent. John was not as convinced as the others about this side of things, but accepted that something had to be put in place to run their affairs now that Brian Epstein was dead. He and George, along with Cynthia and Pattie, were the only two Beatles at the Apple Boutique opening party. The launch was attended by most of London society, but the general public stayed away from the shop in droves and it was not long before it failed.

John and George were still interested in meditation and in the Maharishi, and they did much to popularize his cause amongst young people. They both appeared in public with him several times, including on *The Frost Programme* on ITV, and at a UNICEF gala in Paris.

To all intents and purposes, The Beatles still appeared very much together - at the premiere of John's movie, *How I Won the War*, in London, all four Beatles with their wives and girlfriends attended. In reality, they were all constantly growing further apart and it was not to be long before the differences between them were to become very apparent.

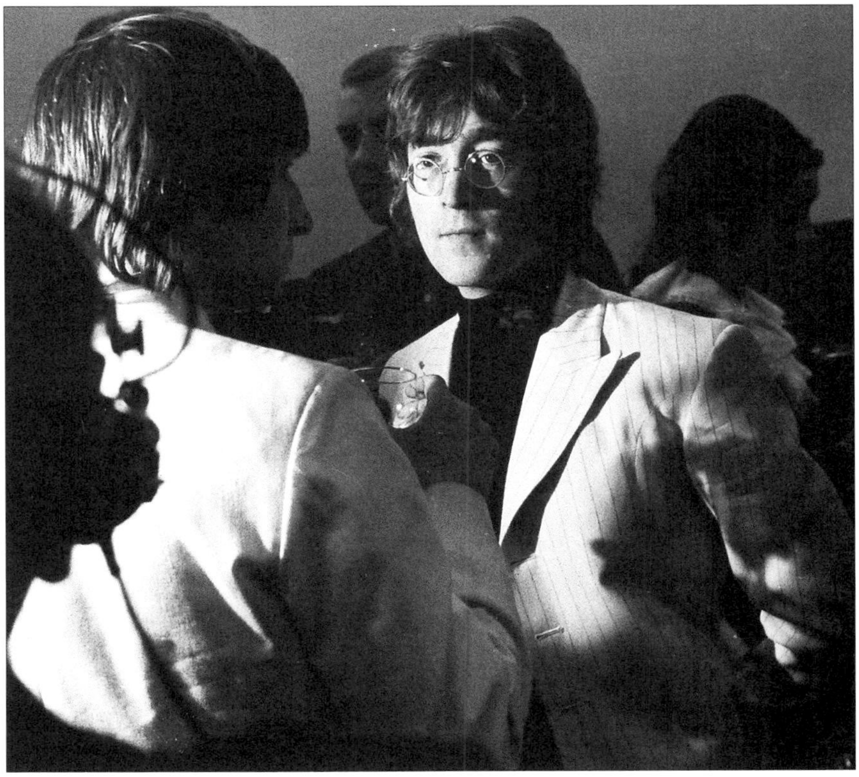

Previous pages: At the party to launch *Sgt. Pepper*, John sports the latest in psychedelic gear.

Right: John at the opening party for the Apple Boutique in Baker Street, London. The shop is described as 'a psychedelic Garden of Eden for lovers of hippy gear, but although all London's glitterati turn out for the party, the buying public refuse to actually buy.

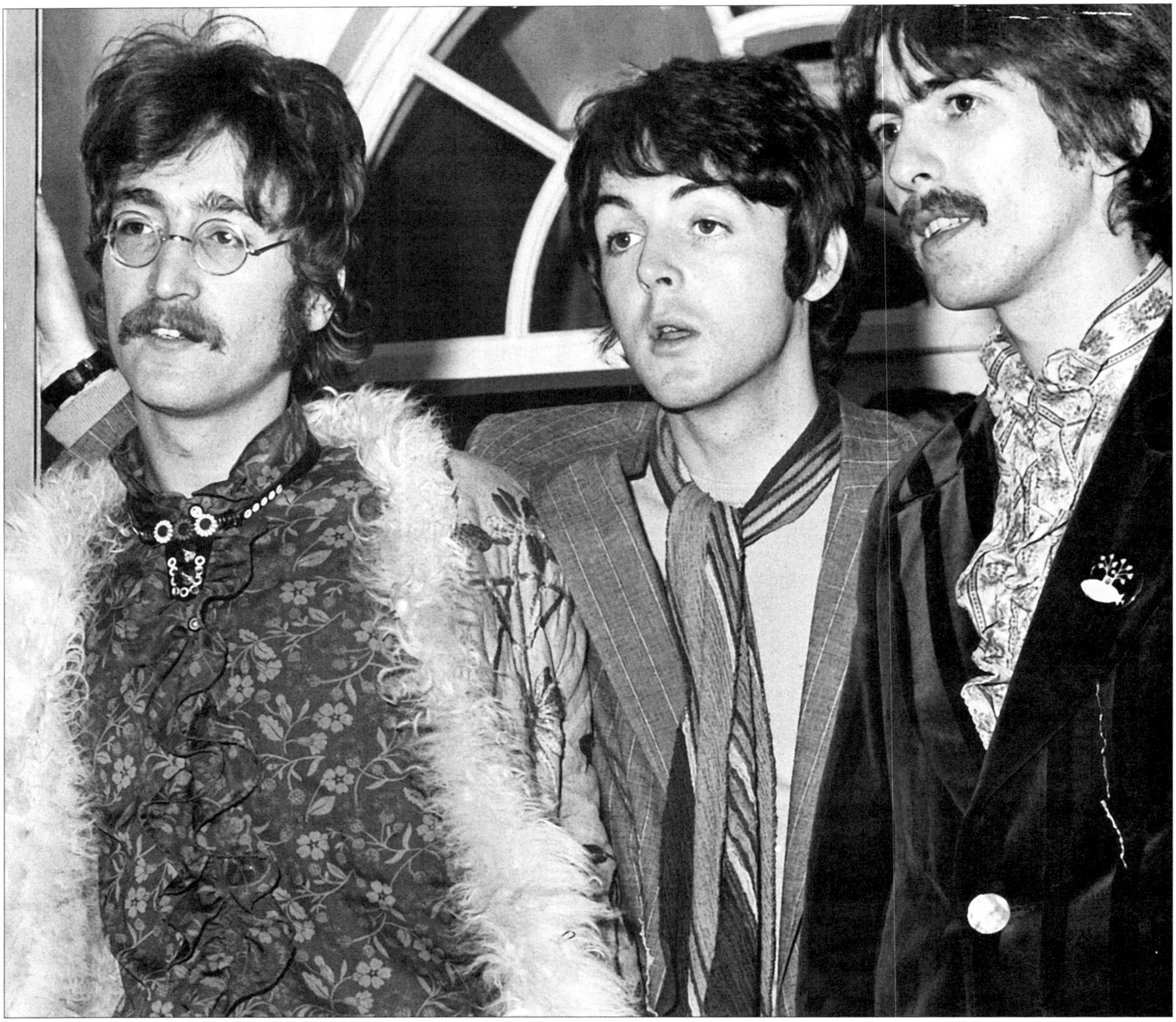

Sgt Pepper's Lonely Hearts Club Band

Previous page: The Beatles appear together to promote the *Sgt. Pepper* LP, revealing the novel gatefold sleeve, printed in full color - and for the first time on a pop or rock album, with all the song lyrics reproduced on the cover.

Whereas the albums *Rubber Soul* and *Revolver* had certainly marked turning points in The Beatles' studio output, 1967's *Sgt. Pepper's Lonely Hearts Club Band* heralded a dramatic shift in popular music, and saw The Beatles recording at their most united - perhaps for the last time.

Above: John, Paul and George at the party Brian Epstein threw to launch *Sgt. Pepper's Lonely Hearts Club Band.* John and Paul had always helped each other out with songs, but *Sgt. Pepper* was the closest The Beatles had ever got to cohesively fulfilling the idea of a concept album. *Sgt. Pepper* was to provide the perfect audio backdrop to the peace, love, art and fashion of the psychedelic summer of '67.

Opposite: The boys at a photo-call at Abbey Road Studios, the day before the *Our World* satellite broadcast.

The Love of My Life

LOVE

Love, Love, Love...

In June The Beatles took part in the world's first televised global satellite link-up, *Our World*, performing the specially composed *All You Need Is Love*. Paul and John both submitted compositions, but it was John's simple and more accessible song that was chosen for the broadcast.

Above: John with his son Julian, at home in Weybridge, Surrey. Although John had been absent for much of his young son's early years, and despite a growing rift between him and Cynthia - exacerbated by his drug intake and Yoko Ono's frequent communications during 1967 - he remained a loving father to Julian.

John's psychedelic Phantom

Above: A beautifully painted gypsy caravan, a present for Julian, arrives outside Kenwood.

Left: John's psychedelic Phantom V Rolls-Royce was formerly a sober, plain black.

Opposite: John at Heathrow Airport with Julian, preparing to leave for a holiday in Greece with Cynthia, Paul McCartney and Paul's girlfriend, actress Jane Asher. Cynthia had tried her best to remain unchanged in order to provide John and their son with some stability, but John was becoming increasingly distant, distracted by drugs and embracing the other-worldliness of psychedelia. Still, the relationship had not yet run its course, and John and Cynthia still found time to be together at home and for the odd holiday abroad.

MORRIS'
237 ELY

All Greek for John

Above: Paul with Julian in Greece.

Opposite: John returning home to England in 'flower power' gear. At about this time John talked the other Beatles into entering negotiations to buy their own Greek island in order to achieve some privacy, but they pulled out of the deal at a fairly early stage.

Custom Cab

ENGINEER
exciting new offer

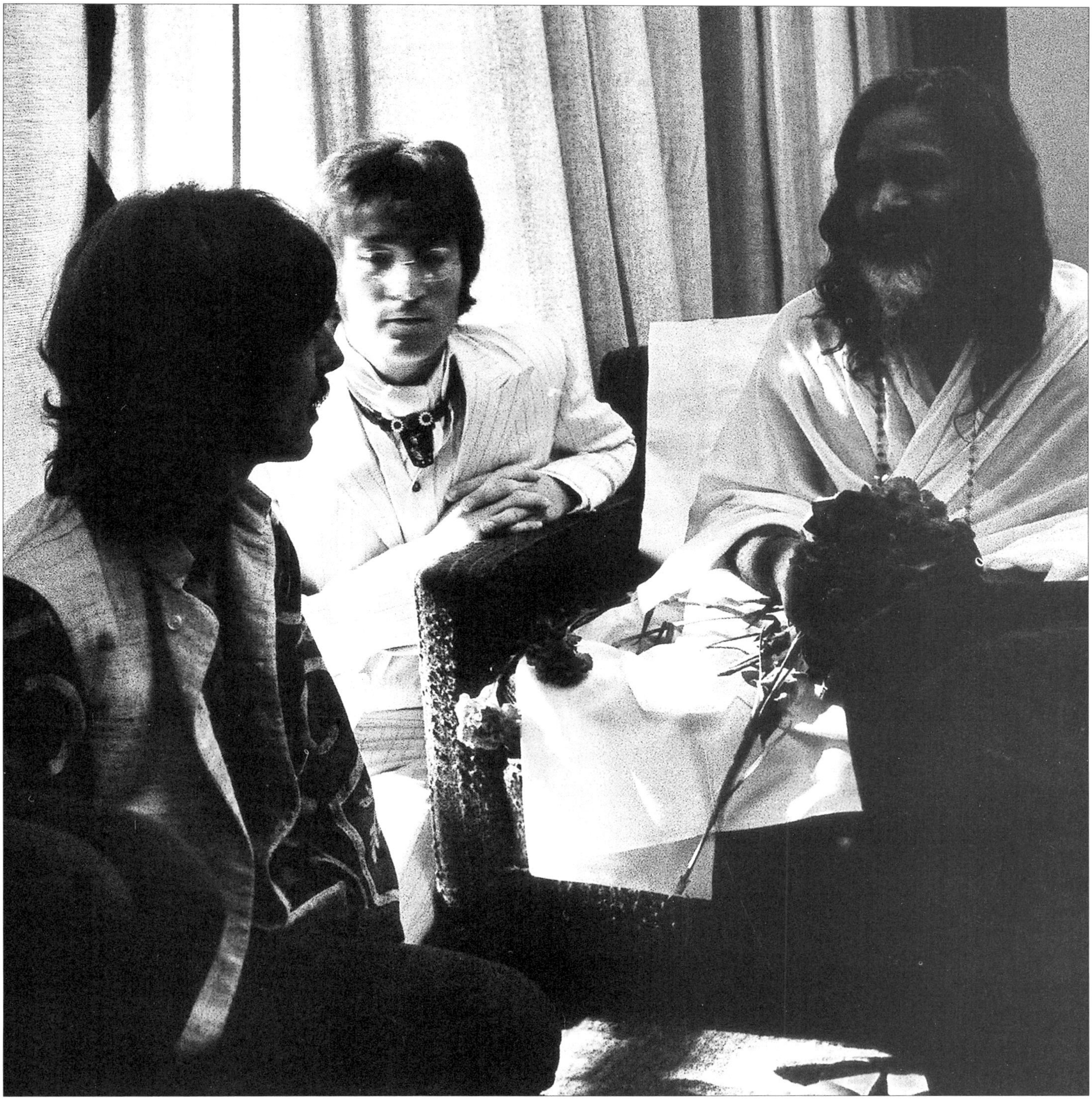

Meeting The Maharishi

The Beatles meet the Maharishi after his lecture at London's Hilton Hotel and are invited to spend the weekend with him at a retreat in Bangor, North Wales. While John had chosen to explore his inner self with the use of drugs, George Harrison had become attracted to Eastern mysticism. When Pattie Harrison saw a poster advertising a lecture on transcendental meditation by the Maharishi Mahesh Yogi, The Beatles were persuaded to attend. John, being at another crossroads in his life, was particularly interested.

Left: Paul and John at London Airport.

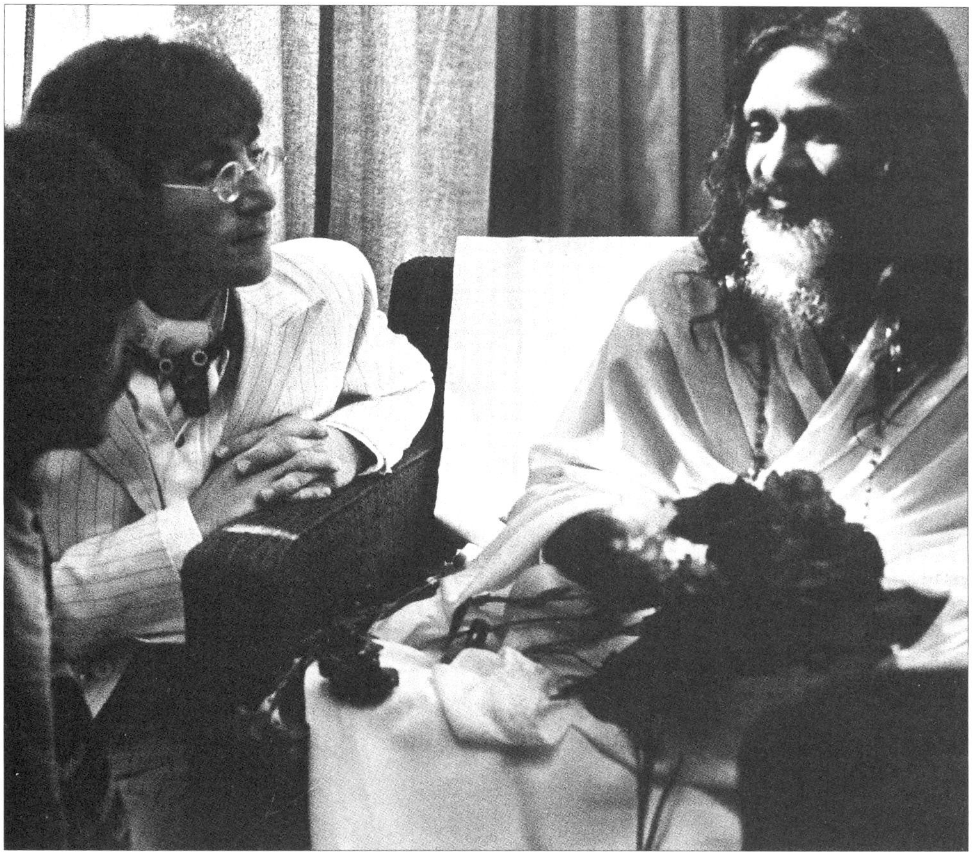

Brian Epstein found dead

Opposite: John on board a train at Euston Station, preparing to leave for Wales. Amidst the commotion of being followed by fans, Cynthia is held back by a policeman and is forced to make her own way there; a moment which was eerily representative of the growing divide between them.

Left and below: John and George were particularly interested in what the Maharishi might have to offer. Brian Epstein was due to join them in Wales, but he was found dead on August 27 in his London home. John was devastated at the news but hid his grief well and remained positive. With his interest in meditation awakened, he likened Brian's death to a passing phase and looked forward to spending some time in India.

The Magical Mystery Tour

Before leaving for India, The Beatles were to throw themselves into another movie project, this time of their own devising - *the Magical Mystery Tour.*

Opposite: John taking a break from filming. *Magical Mystery Tour* took its inspiration from the exploits of Ken Kesey and The Merry Pranksters who had toured California in a psychedelic bus in 1965, freely distributing LSD. The plot was minimal and The Beatles hoped that events would unfold naturally as they toured the English countryside.

Roll up for the Mystery Tour

Right: John on location in the West Country. *The Magical Mystery Tour* project was, however, beset by problems from the outset, and after its Boxing Day broadcast it was panned by the British Press. John himself was later to dismiss the movie, saying The Beatles felt that they 'owed it to the public to do these things'.

Above: John makes a stop during filming to sign autographs in Plymouth.

How I Won The War

Opposite: John on The Beatles' magic bus. *The Magical Mystery Tour* was essentially Paul's project and although John was going along with it, he resented Paul's attempt to take charge of the group.

Above: Three Beatles in serious mode. As far as John was concerned, after Brian Epstein's death The Beatles were finished.

Right: John and Cynthia arrive at the London Pavilion on October 18 for the première of John's movie, *How I Won The War.*

Apple

John and Cynthia arrive with the Harrisons to celebrate the opening of the Apple Boutique in Baker Street, London, in December. Following Epstein's death The Beatles opted to manage their own affairs, and undaunted by the relative failure of *Magical Mystery Tour*, launched themselves into various business enterprises. The first of these was the Apple Boutique, a shop selling 'beautiful things for beautiful people'.

Above: John and Cynthia take up front row seats for the première of *How I Won The War*, accompanied by all the other Beatles and their partners.

RESTAURANT

The Beatles & Co.

Although the launch party went well, the boutique itself was to prove rather less successful, closing after only seven months of business with the remaining stock being given away. Ironically, the give-away attracted massive crowds who fought to get into the store now that it was closing.

As well as Apple, John, Paul, George and Ringo had recently formed The Beatles & Co., a legal partnership to handle all their business affairs, which bound them together until 1977. Unfortunately, this was to prove a major and costly mistake within only a few years.

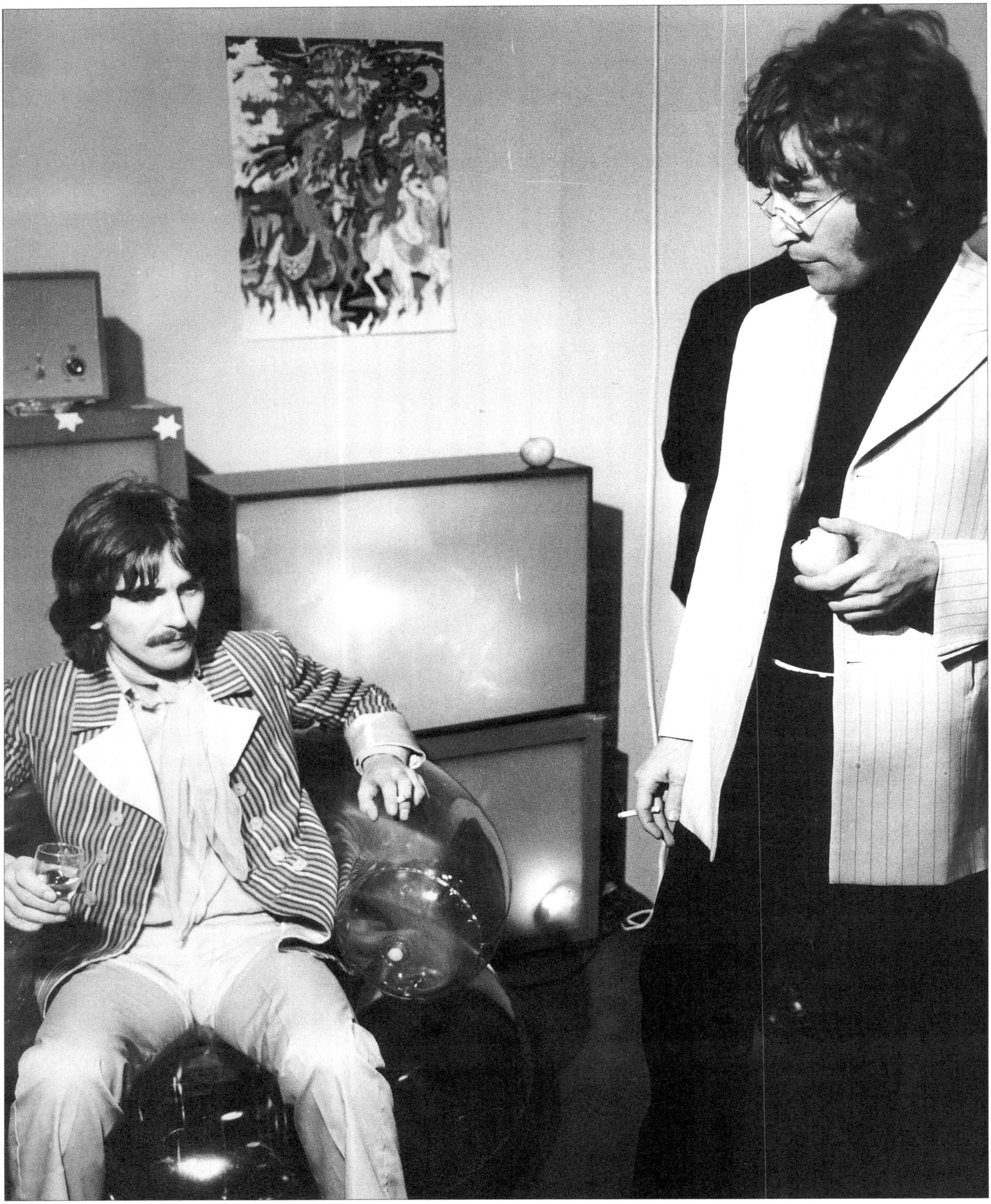

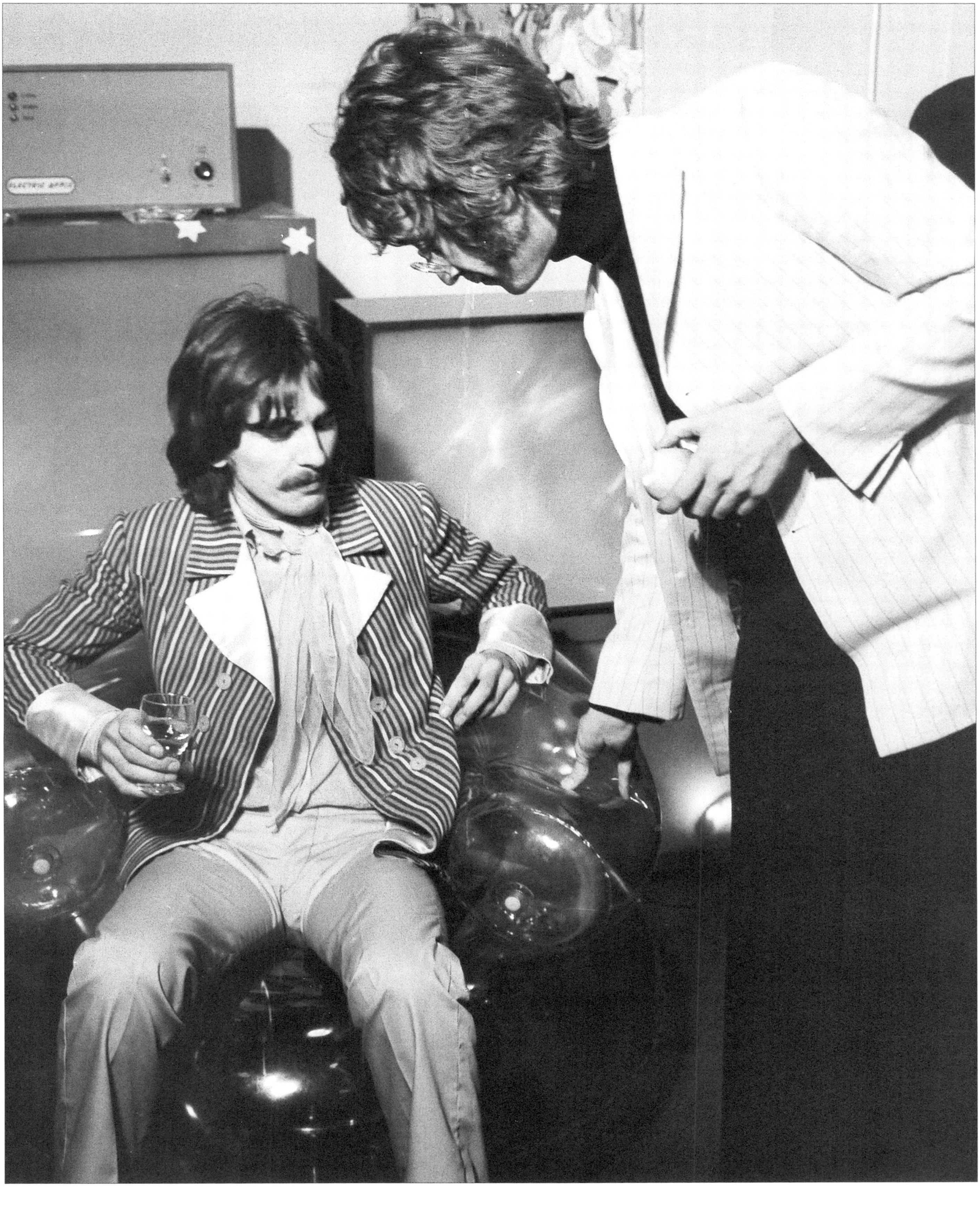

Buttons
Buttons

An Apple a Day

The Beatles planned to build their own empire in which they would be in total control. As well as handling their own business, the Apple organization was intended to operate philanthropically to foster new talent - although John was never convinced that this would work in practise.

Previous pages: John and George relax at the launch party for their Apple Boutique.

Yoko exhibition at Lisson Gallery

Above: John at another party, this time at an art exhibition in London. In October, an exhibition of Yoko's work had opened at London's Lisson Art Gallery. It was called *Half-Wind Show*, and it consisted of several everyday objects all cut in half. The show was subtitled *Yoko plus Me*: the 'Me' was John, who had sponsored it, but insisted on remaining anonymous and did not attend.

Opposite: George and John at the Apple launch party.

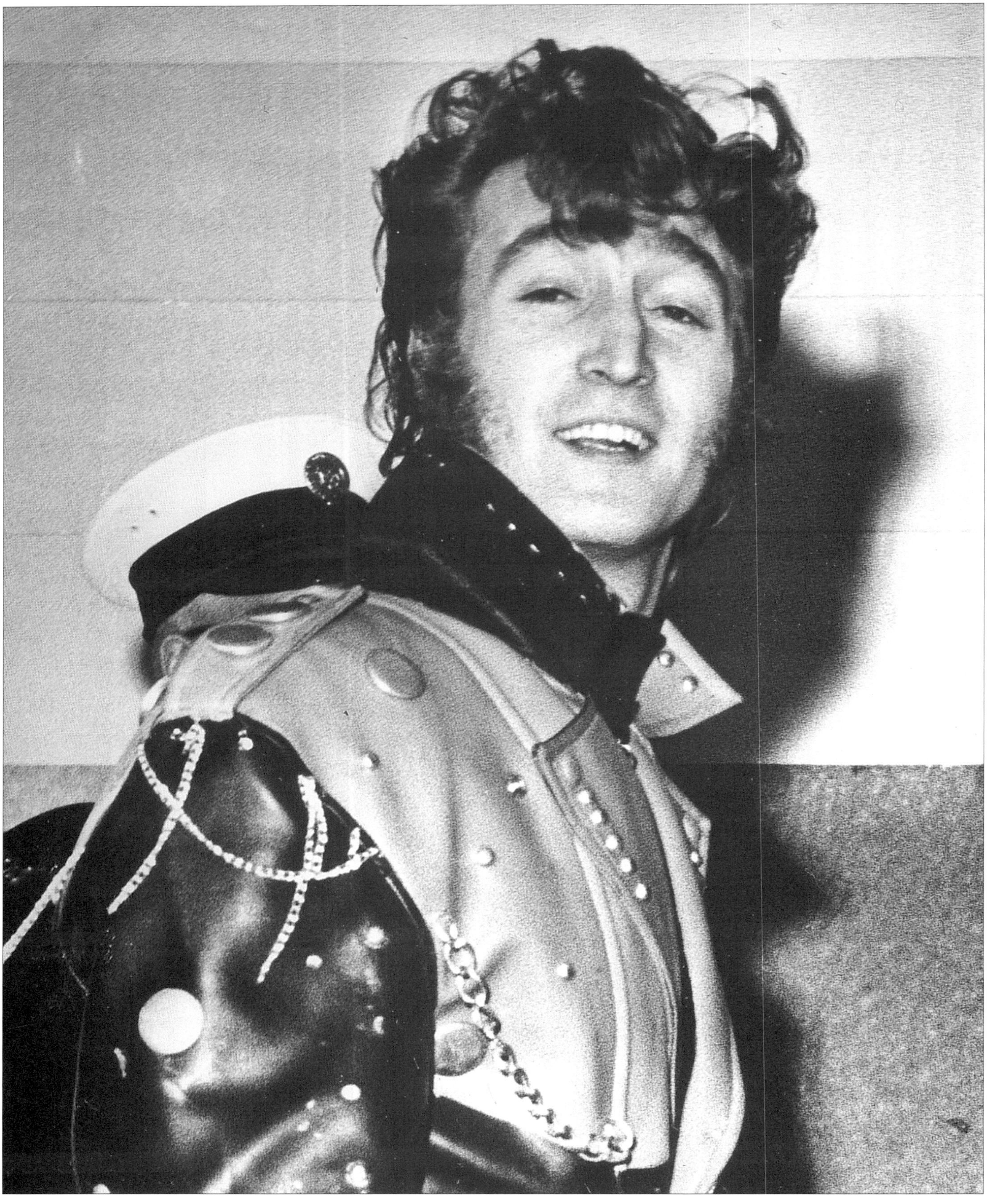

CHAPTER SIX

1968 I'm so tired

At the beginning of 1968, Fred Lennon turned up at John's home in Weybridge again. He had met nineteen-year-old former student Pauline Jones, and the two of them wanted to get married. Unfortunately her mother was very much set against the idea, and had made her daughter a ward of court. John found a job for Pauline temporarily as his secretary, allowed her to stay in his home and later paid for their wedding in Scotland, which was out of the English court's jurisdiction. Later he bought the couple a house in Kew, and finally established a workable if not close relationship with his father.

In February, John and Cynthia flew out to the Himalayan retreat of the Maharishi Mahesh Yogi in India to attend a three-month course in transcendental meditation. They were accompanied by George and Pattie and the other two Beatles and their partners followed a few days later. Ringo and Maureen had had enough after less than two weeks, while Paul and Jane left after five. John and George stayed for almost two months, before becoming disillusioned with the Maharishi's character and methods - although not with his basic message.

Soon after their return to England, John and Paul went to New York for five days, where John took the opportunity to denounce the Maharishi, while appearing on NBC's *Tonight Show*. However, the real reason for their trip was to announce the formation of Apple Corps Ltd. The new company was to have different divisions covering areas such as music, movies, electronics, merchandise and the arts, and one of its functions was to invest funds to help creative people start out. This was supposed to be run on a business footing, so that at some point there would be a return on the investment. John and Paul took it all very seriously and went into Apple's offices every day to direct operations. However, since no one appeared to check whether funds going out would ever bring any sort of return, Apple soon became a source of easy money to anyone who knocked on the door. The company executives and staff also took full advantage of the situation, giving themselves lavish salaries and large expense accounts. One employee later described working there as being 'the longest cocktail party', but for some time neither John nor the others realized what was going on.

John was still fascinated by Yoko, who had written to him regularly while he was away in India. In May, he invited her to his home while Cynthia was away on holiday and the two of them sat up all night experimenting with sounds and recording music and voices, and had then finally gone to bed. From that moment on it was inevitable that they would be together. Although Cynthia came home to find Yoko there, initially John refused to face up to the situation and make the break, so he and Cynthia carried on living together for another few weeks.

Cynthia soon left again for Italy on a prearranged holiday with Julian and her mother, and while she was away John and Yoko began to appear in public together. When the two of them planted acorns in the grounds of Coventry Cathedral as part of the National Sculpture Exhibition, it could just have been seen as a natural progression of John's interest in art. The acorns were supposed to represent East and West, symbolizing the meeting of two different cultures. However, when they arrived hand-in-hand at the London première of *In His Own Write*, a play based on John's two books, there was no concealing the situation any longer and journalists had a field day. They called out to John, asking him where his wife was, and pictures of him and Yoko appeared in most of the national papers. Cynthia saw them in Italy and knew that her marriage was over; by the end of the year she and John were divorced.

Now John and Yoko were openly together, he became even more publicly involved with the art world. In July, the first exhibition of his own work, *You Are Here*, opened in the Robert Fraser Gallery in central London. It consisted of a display of fifty charity collecting boxes and was dedicated to Yoko. Before the opening, he and Yoko, both dressed all in white, released 365 helium-filled balloons over London. Although Yoko was still married to American film director Anthony Cox, she was also now heading for divorce.

Despite his new interests, John still had commitments from the past to fulfill. The original deal that had been done with United Artists meant that one more Beatles movie had to be made. None of them had been particularly interested in doing it, but they had agreed on a full-length animated movie to be based on one of their earlier songs, which was two years in the making; *Yellow Submarine* was finally released in 1968. Although The Beatles had been consulted about the concept at the beginning, they had not been involved in developing the storyline and even the voice-overs were done by actors. However, they did write four new songs for the soundtrack and film a short cameo appearance, which was inserted near the end. The movie was poorly distributed in Britain, but did extremely well in America and it was very highly regarded by the critics - later it was often dubbed 'the best movie The Beatles never made'.The group turned out in force for the London première of *Yellow Submarine* in July, but this time John was again accompanied by Yoko.

One unexpected advantage of The Beatles' long stay in India was that it had removed them from their usual environments and given both John and Paul ample time to write new songs - and George had also been hard at work. They had returned with enough material for a new album, so they soon went into the studio to begin recording their double LP, *The Beatles* - which soon became known as the *White Album* to distinguish it from the name of the band. However, problems soon surfaced. John and Paul did not really like each other's new songs, while George felt his material was constantly being dismissed. On top of this, Yoko was now ever present in the studio, whispering to John, encouraging his ideas - and actually daring to criticize and comment on the work in progress. Until then outsiders had been banned and wives and girlfriends had only been allowed to watch from the control room, so the other Beatles bitterly resented Yoko's presence on the studio floor. The tension became so bad that Ringo, always the most easy-going of the four, walked out - thus technically becoming the first Beatle to leave the group, although he was talked into returning just over a week later.

Although it was common knowledge that The Beatles had experimented with drugs, as did many other well-known pop artistes at the time, until now there had been no official move against any of them. In October that year, however, John and Yoko were awoken early in the morning by police with dogs at the door of the apartment they shared in Montagu Square. After a thorough search, a small piece of cannabis was found and they were arrested and charged. John later maintained that it was a set-up - he had been tipped off by a journalist that the police were taking an interest and had cleaned the flat out, so he was sure that the drugs had been planted. However, he pleaded guilty to protect Yoko - even though he knew a conviction might cause problems if he wanted to visit America. He was fined £150 and ordered to paytwenty guineas costs.

By now Yoko was several months pregnant, with her baby due the following February. The announcement hastened John's divorce through the courts - until then he had been maintaining that he had not been unfaithful in an attempt to minimize the settlement due to Cynthia. Unfortunately Yoko miscarried the following month; John stayed with her at the hospital, sleeping first in the next bed and then on the floor, but refusing to leave her side.

At the end of November, John and Yoko released their first album together, *Unfinished Music No. 1: Two Virgins*, a collection of strange sounds and musical effects, most of which had been recorded back in May during that first evening together at John's house in Weybridge. John decided the two of them should be photographed nude for the front and back of the sleeve, so EMI declined to distribute the record and it was released through Apple. It was not only panned by the critics but was also a commercial failure on both sides of the Atlantic - and thousands of copies were impounded and confiscated by Customs as indecent. John was not concerned - the record had been released as a statement rather than as a commercial venture.

In December, John and Yoko both appeared on stage at the Royal Albert Hall concealed in a large white bag for *Alchemical Wedding*, the underground art world's Christmas party, and they distributed presents together at the Apple Christmas party, John dressed as Santa Claus and Yoko as Mother Christmas. John was rapidly losing interest in doing anything with The Beatles - he wanted to move forward artistically with Yoko. However, something urgently needed to be done about Apple Corps, which had spent more than £1 million but made nothing in return. The boutique in Baker Street had closed; when all the left-over stock was given away it was the first time crowds fought to get into the store. The other Beatles still seemed unaware of the problem, but despite his laid-back demeanor John had always had a surprisingly sharp business brain and he soon blew the whistle on what was going on.

Page 218: John arrives at a fancy dress party in London at the Royal Lancaster Hotel.

Apple and grapefruit

After launching the Apple Boutique, The Beatles established the Apple record label, signing the band Grapefruit. The Press conference to launch the group's first single 'Dear Delilah' was held at the Hanover Grand in London, and amongst those in attendance were The Beatles, Brian Jones, Donovan and Cilla Black.

Right: John and Cynthia at a fashion show, in which George's wife Pattie is modeling Although it was Paul who was always the most publicly sociable Beatle, John frequently attended exhibitions and parties throughout the latter half of the 1960s.

John and the Maharishi

At the Maharishi's retreat in Rishikesh, everybody lived in concrete chalets and followed a routine of meditation, chanting and communal praying. Ringo and Maureen had had enough after a few days, and they were followed by Paul and Jane not long afterwards. John and Cynthia stayed several weeks longer, along with George and Patti, but eventually they all became very disillusioned with the Maharishi himself.

Opposite: John had appeared several times in public to endorse the Maharishi and his movement, but after leaving India he was quick to denounce his former mentor.

Apple… in the Big Apple…

After returning from Rishikesh John got back to business, flying to New York with Paul to announce the formation of Apple Corps Ltd, the umbrella organization for all their business ventures.

John and Paul spent five days in New York, but despite John's involvement in Apple, he was becoming increasingly disenchanted with Paul, as he perceived him to be attempting to fulfill the role once played by Brian Epstein.

If no one
claims me in
30 days
I'M YOURS

First public appearance with Yoko

While in India, John had become more distant from Cynthia and had decided to focus on developing his relationship with Yoko Ono, inviting her to Kenwood while Cynthia was on vacation in Greece. Throughout his marriage John had been involved with other women, but in Yoko he was immediately convinced that he had found 'The One'. They made their first public appearance in May 1968 at a party and Press conference for a second Apple Boutique, closely followed by an 'event' where they planted acorns outside Coventry Cathedral. However the Press only sat up and took notice when they attended the London opening of *In His Own Write* in June.

John And Yoko

John and Yoko with actor Victor Spinetti, who had adapted *In His Own Write* from John's first two books.

Opposite: John's first art exhibition, *You Are Here*, opens on July 1 in Mayfair. The exhibition is dedicated to Yoko and consists of fifty charity boxes.

You Are Here

John and Yoko attend *You Are Here* in matching white outfits, instead of their usual dark attire.

The exhibition opens with the release of 365 helium-filled balloons and John publicly declares his love for Yoko - who is also still married, to American director Anthony Cox.

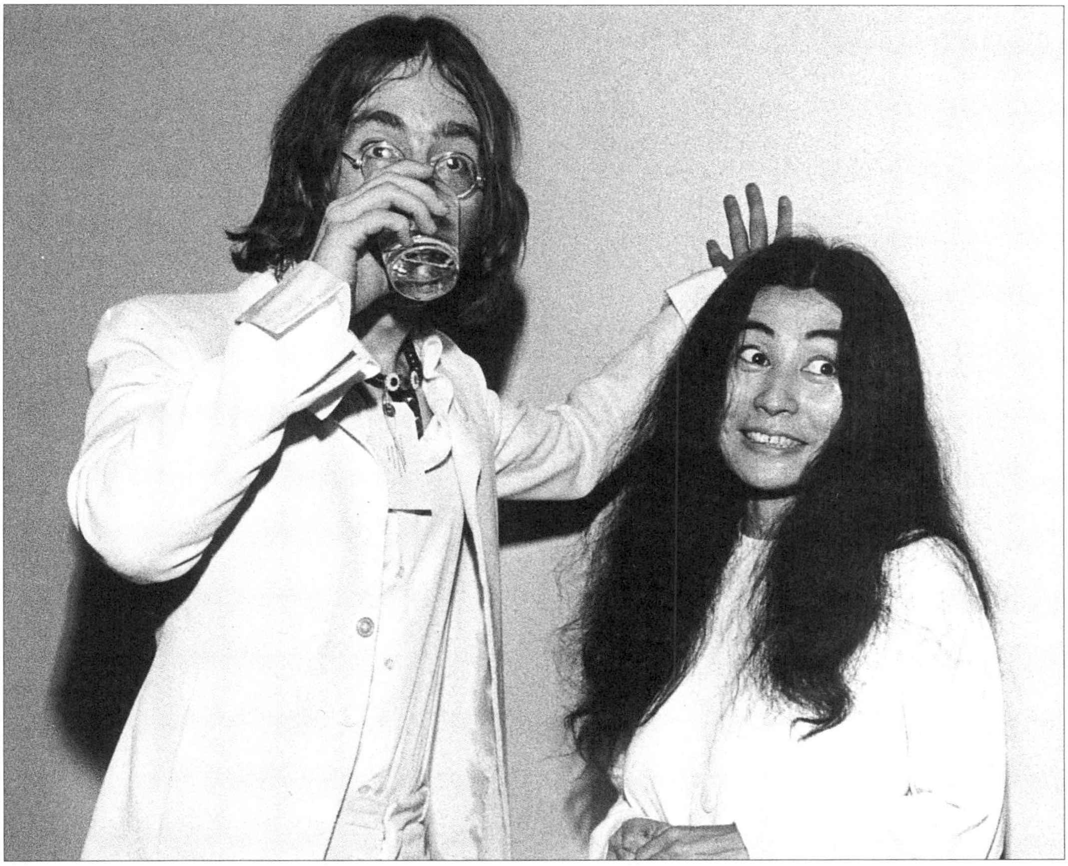

Yellow Submarine

John and Paul at the London première of *Yellow Submarine.* Owing to contractual obligations The Beatles were required to release another movie in 1968, resulting in the animated *Yellow Submarine.* Their contribution was minimal though, as they provided only four new songs and appeared briefly in a live-action sequence near the end of the movie.

Opposite: In 1968 The Beatles waxworks receive another makeover - their fifth - and new clothing, to keep up with their changing image.

Divorce

Cynthia at the Royal Courts of Justice in London in November 1968, the month when she was finally divorced from John. Following some acrimonious scenes at Kenwood, John had moved into a apartment owned by Ringo in Montagu Square, London, with the woman whom he had once dismissed to his wife as 'that weird artist'. Cynthia filed for divorce on the grounds of John's adultery.

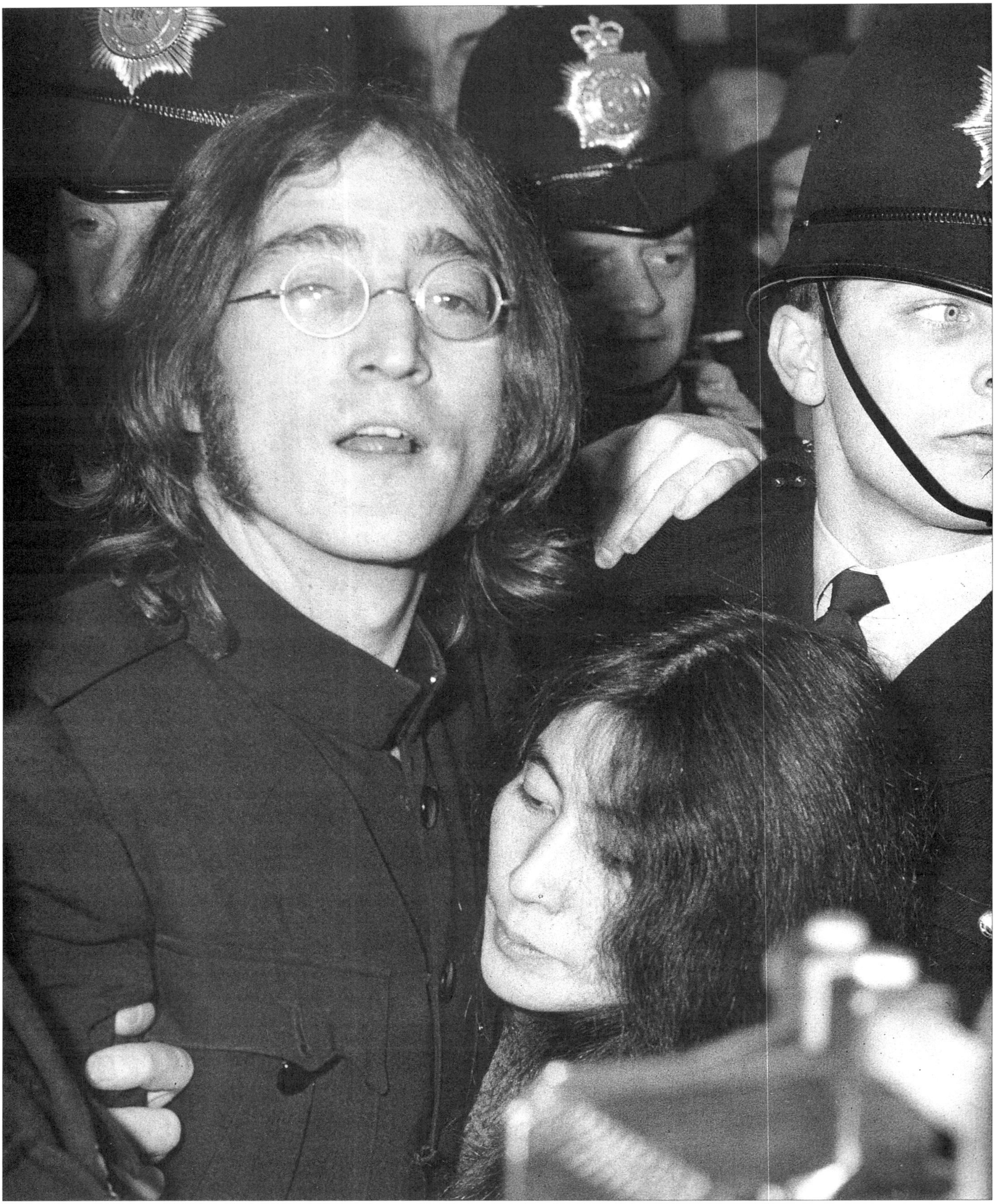

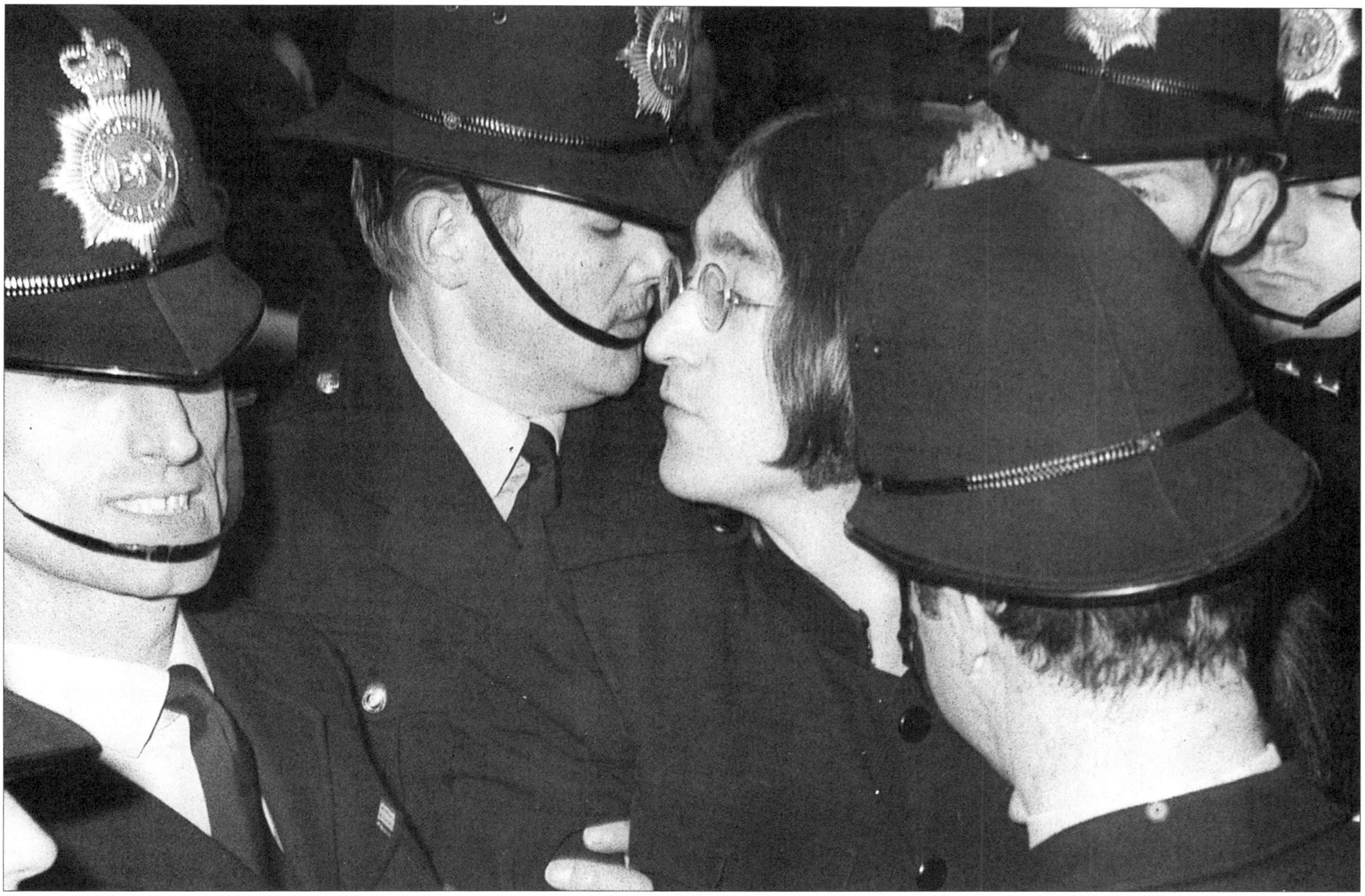

A testing time for John and Yoko

Early on October 18, the Montagu Square apartment now occupied by John and Yoko was raided by police and a small quantity of cannabis was seized. They were arrested and charged with obstruction and possession of cannabis, and remanded on bail to reappear later that month. They both knew that a drugs conviction could prove problematic if they wished to return to America in the future.

From bad to worse for John and Yoko

John maintained that he had been set up, but pleaded guilty in November in order to protect Yoko, who was not a British citizen and so was in danger of deportation. John was fined £150 for the possession of cannabis, but charges against Yoko were subsequently dropped. To make things worse, amidst mounting pressures from both within The Beatles' camp and outside it, their happiness that Yoko was pregnant was to be shattered by a miscarriage over the course of their trial.

Rock and Roll Circus

Yoko and John with Julian, watching a rehearsal of The Rolling Stones' *Rock and Roll Circus*, a planned television show which was to feature many stars, including John himself.

TRIUM
HIWAT

Rocking with Brian and Keith

Yoko, John and Julian with Brian Jones of the Rolling Stones on the set of *Rock and Roll Circus.*

Opposite: John waiting to perform at Intertel film studios, Wembley. Keith Richards of the Rolling Stones is behind him.

CHAPTER SEVEN

1969
Love is old, love is new

At the beginning of January, The Beatles assembled at Twickenham Studios to be filmed rehearsing, as part of a documentary that was to show them preparing for either a television broadcast or a concert. Almost immediately the tensions between them surfaced - they are clearly apparent in the final movie, *Let it Be*. This time George walked out and although he was persuaded to return the idea of a concert was shelved. When The Beatles played live at the end of January on the roof of the Apple building, which was filmed for *Let it Be*, it was the last time they performed together as a group. Meanwhile, they went back to the studio to record an LP, but although the final tapes were not up to their usual high standard none of them could face further work on it. Instead they decided to start afresh - and this time produced *Abbey Road*, one of their best LPs.

John had been concerned about the state of Apple Corps for some time, but early that year he went public, telling *Disc and Music Echo* that he and the others had made a big mistake with Apple, and that they now realized they were not businessmen. He went on to say, '...if it carries on like this all of us will be broke in the next six months'. Paul was furious that John had spoken to the Press, although he accepted that there were problems that needed to be addressed. However, the four of them could not all agree on who should be appointed to come in and sort things out. John and Yoko wanted Allen Klein, a tough New York show-business lawyer, who had been introduced to them by the Rolling Stones, and they eventually convinced George and Ringo. Paul didn't trust Klein and wanted the New York firm of Eastman & Eastman - run by his girlfriend Linda's father and brother - but John and the others felt the Eastmans would only be looking out for Paul's best interests. John and Yoko prevailed and Klein's company, ABKCO, was appointed - it was the first time The Beatles had done anything without all four members being in agreement.

Another business problem also now came to a head - the group lost their controlling interest in Brian

Epstein's old company, NEMS, and in Northern Songs, the company that published their songs. This meant they no longer owned the rights to any of their compositions and valuable royalties were going to other people. Klein failed to stop it happening - although he did achieve a much better royalty deal from EMI for the group's American sales.

Yoko's divorce from Anthony Cox had come through in February, so she and John were finally able to marry in March. At the time they were based in Paris, but decided to charter a plane and fly to Gibraltar to get married at the British Consulate. Both of them wore white for the wedding - as John said, they were 'tremendous romantics'. They spent just over an hour in Gibraltar, before flying back to Paris, but told the Press to look out for another 'happening'. Journalists did not have long to wait - a few days later the happy couple took over the presidential suite at the Amsterdam Hilton, and announced they were planning to stay in bed together for seven days. They invited the Press, and journalists from around the world turned up to find John and Yoko dressed in white and surrounded by flowers, with notices pinned up saying 'Bed Peace' and 'Hair Peace'. John urged everyone to stay in bed and grow their hair, instead of being violent. It became the first of several 'bed-ins' for peace, and they also came up with several other ideas to catch the attention of the Press. At the end of March their movie, *Rape*, was premièred on Austrian television, and at a brief Press conference in Vienna John and Yoko publicly launched 'bagism', another manifestation of their peace campaign. They appeared on stage together inside a large white bag and refused to emerge, although they happily answered questions. One benefit of 'bagism', John explained, was that no one could be distracted from their message by the color of their skin, or the length of their hair.

As John became more involved with Yoko, he found that he developed different ideas about many things. She pointed out how unfair it was that she had had to change her name when they married, so he decided to change his too. At an official ceremony on the roof of the Apple building, he became John Ono Lennon - although he never entirely managed to get rid of his original middle name, Winston, legally. The two of them soon bought a home together as well - Tittenhurst Park, where the last photo of all four Beatles together was taken later that year.

Although he was no longer interested in performing with The Beatles, John had by no means given up music. He soon released a second LP with Yoko, *Unfinished Music No 2. - Life with the Lions.* Musically it was not a great success, but that was not the point - he just wanted to continue experimenting and push the boundaries even further.

Although John's application for a US visa had been rejected because of his 1968 drugs conviction, Canada proved more welcoming and another bed-in for peace was staged at a hotel in Montreal. While there, a makeshift group of friends and acquaintances - which was christened the Plastic Ono Band - recorded a new song John had written, 'Give Peace a Chance'. It was one of his most successful compositions and went on to become the anthem for the peace movement.

Despite the excitement of his new life, John felt guilty about abandoning Julian and continued to see him regularly, just as Yoko tried to spend time with Kyoko. In July the two of them took both children for a weekend in Scotland, where John hired car. He was not a good driver and he badly misjudged a bend and rolled off the road into a ditch; he and Yoko were badly cut, Kyoko was slightly injured and Julian suffered from shock. They were taken to the local hospital where John, Yoko and Kyoko all had to have sutures and were kept in for several days. Julian was fine, but Cynthia quickly arrived to collect him and take him back to London.

Soon afterwards John and Yoko were supposed to be appearing at the launch of the Plastic Ono Band in London, but since they were still in hospital their stand-ins were a pair of Perspex tubes fitted with microphones, tape recorders and amplifiers. John felt it was very symbolic, showing the world that the Plastic Ono Band was a conceptual band with no actual members. However, they soon began releasing records - beginning with John's first solo single, 'Give Peace a Chance'. In September, the Plastic Ono Band was invited to perform at a concert in Toronto. John called up several old friends, including Eric Clapton and Klaus Voormann, just the night before; they rehearsed in the plane on the way over. John loved this kind of spontaneity, even if the final result was rather raw - he found the endless polishing to perfection done on The Beatles' songs laborious and boring. On the way to Toronto John decided finally that he wanted to quit The Beatles and told his companions. He later told Klein as well, but was persuaded to keep it quiet for the moment because negotiations with EMI to achieve an increased offer were at a delicate stage.

The peace campaign was doing well, but John decided that it needed an extra push and even more publicity. He sent his chauffeur to 'borrow' his MBE back from Mimi - who was horrified to read in the papers the following day that he had returned it to the Queen. He enclosed a note, explaining that he was protesting against Britain's involvement in Biafra, America's involvement in Vietnam - and against his current record slipping down the charts. He later explained to the Press that he had always felt uncomfortable about accepting the honor, but that he had done so because it was expected of a Beatle. Now he was rejecting it to draw attention to the peace campaign - and the reference to his record was a joke, so the Queen wouldn't think his letter was from 'some boring colonel'.

Before the end of the year he and Yoko were to take up yet another cause - they were introduced to the parents of James Hanratty, a convicted murderer who had been hanged in Britain in 1962. They soon became convinced of his innocence and began to take every opportunity to demonstrate on his behalf. At the end of one of the most eventful years in his life, John felt he was finally beginning to get through to people. A poll in *Disc and Music Echo* not only named him the most popular Beatle, but revealed most readers were coming round to his views. Even the mainstream media had stopped treating him as if he was a joke - at the end of December he was featured in a three-part program on ITV, *Man of the Decade*, along with John F. Kennedy and Mao Tse Tung.

The Rolling Stones' Rock And Roll Circus

Both John and Yoko were invited to participate in the television special hosted by the Rolling Stones. The show remained incomplete and was never broadcast, but John contributed 'Yer Blues' with 'The Dirty Mac', alongside Keith Richards, Mitch Mitchell and Eric Clapton, and 'Whole Lotta Yoko' with 'The Dirty Mac' and Yoko Ono.

For sale

Left: John's white Rolls Royce, reflected in the window at Kenwood. Now divorced from Cynthia, and with too many memories at the house, John began looking for a new home for himself and Yoko.

Below left: John's chess set, all in white.

Below: A close-up of Kenwood's somewhat suggestive doorknocker.

Opposite: A haunted look performing in *The Rolling Stones' Rock And Roll Circus.*

John: 'I hope we passed the audition'

In January 1969 The Beatles set about filming rehearsals with a view to producing a performance for television. Originally entitled *Get Back*, the project became *Let It Be*, a documentary account cum feature film of the recording of a new album. The final film included the last live performance by The Beatles, on the roof of the Apple offices in London. At the end of the impromptu show, surrounded by a small audience gathered on the rooftop, and with crowds blocking the streets below, John remarked, 'I'd like to thank you on behalf of the group and ourselves and I hope we passed the audition'.

Above: John's bedroom at Kenwood, with its huge bed. John became a keen purchaser of books during his time there, and many can be seen at his bedside and on the windowsill. Also notable is a picture of John and Yoko on the right.

From Paris to the Amsterdam Hilton…

On March 20, 1969, John and Yoko flew from Paris to Gibraltar where they were married at the British Consulate. They returned immediately to Paris where they remained for a few days before flying to Amsterdam and beginning a week-long 'bed-in' at the Amsterdam Hilton. The couple remained in their hotel room, in bed, for a week, where they launched a peace campaign to the world's Press.

Strengthened by his unity with Yoko, John was no longer to suppress his avant-garde tendencies, or his disaffection with political aggression, such as the conflict in Vietnam. Many regarded the 'bed-in' as no more than a stunt, but John Lennon as the political artist and humanitarian campaigner was now realized and revealed.

Bed peace, hair peace

During the week in Amsterdam nearly 100 reporters from around the world came to see the Lennons in bed. The couple urged everyone to stay in bed and grow their hair instead of fighting, and were delighted that their message was broadcast all round the world - even if most of the Press thought they were totally mad.

Rape

On March 31, John and Yoko travelled from Amsterdam to the Austrian capital, Vienna, in order to witness the TV première of their movie, *Rape*. The movie is a parody of the effects of media intrusion, depicting the constant pursuit of a girl by a camera crew, whom she eventually attacks. The parallels with John's own experiences were obvious, and *Rape* was seen as highly confrontational. John and Yoko then held a Press conference in their hotel in Vienna, covered by a white sheet.

Peace movement

John and Yoko arrive at Heathrow Airport from Vienna on April 1, making their way to the Press lounge to face the British camera crews. John's involvement with the peace movement came at a time when he desperately needed something to distract him from the growing problems of The Beatles, and he threw himself into the movement with typical enthusiasm.

passenge

Acorns for peace

After the campaign against them in the Press earlier, John and Yoko were surprised to be welcomed home by interviewers in England. At a Press conference they urged people to plant acorns as part of their campaign for peace, explaining that they would be sending pairs of acorns to world leaders and asking them to do the same.

Two cultures

John and Yoko display some of the acorns they plan to send out. Right at the start of their relationship on June 15, 1968, the two of them had planted acorns in the grounds of Coventry Cathedral as part of the National Sculpture Exhibition. The acorns were supposed to represent east and west, symbolizing the meeting of two different cultures.

BAGISM

Beneath a sheet

Opposite: Also on April 1, John and Yoko appear on Thames Television's Today program presented by Eamonn Andrews, promoting '*Bagism*', and convincing the host to join them beneath a sheet.

Above: Yoko in the large kitchen at Tittenhurst Park, a Georgian mansion in Berkshire which John bought in May 1969. With typical irreverence - but perhaps also with some truth, considering his plans for the building of a home recording studio and dreams of a tranquil existence - John describes the vast house and its seventy-two acres, as 'functional'.

TWA
TWA

Kyoko

Prior to moving into their new home, John and Yoko were joined in May by Yoko's daughter Kyoko, who flew in from New York alone. They spent some time in London, before visiting the Bahamas where John hoped to stage another 'bed-in', having been refused a visa to enter the US. Just one day later, however, owing to the punishing humidity of the Bahamas and a desire to be closer to the States, they left for Canada where they staged another seven-day 'bed-in' at the Queen Elizabeth Hotel, Montreal.

Opposite and below: John and Yoko meet Kyoko at Heathrow airport.

Recording with Yoko

Opposite: Kyoko visits the Apple offices in London with John and Yoko, where they are presented with a bunch of carnations by a fan. John spent a great deal of time at the Apple HQ over this period, attempting to resolve financial and legal disputes. Meanwhile in the studio, he continued to work both on material from the *Get Back* project, both with and without the other Beatles, and on new recordings with Yoko.

Left: John, Yoko and Kyoko in London just before leaving for the Bahamas.

Below: John, George, Ringo and their respective partners attend the Isle of Wight festival in September, where they see Bob Dylan perform.

PRIVATE EYE

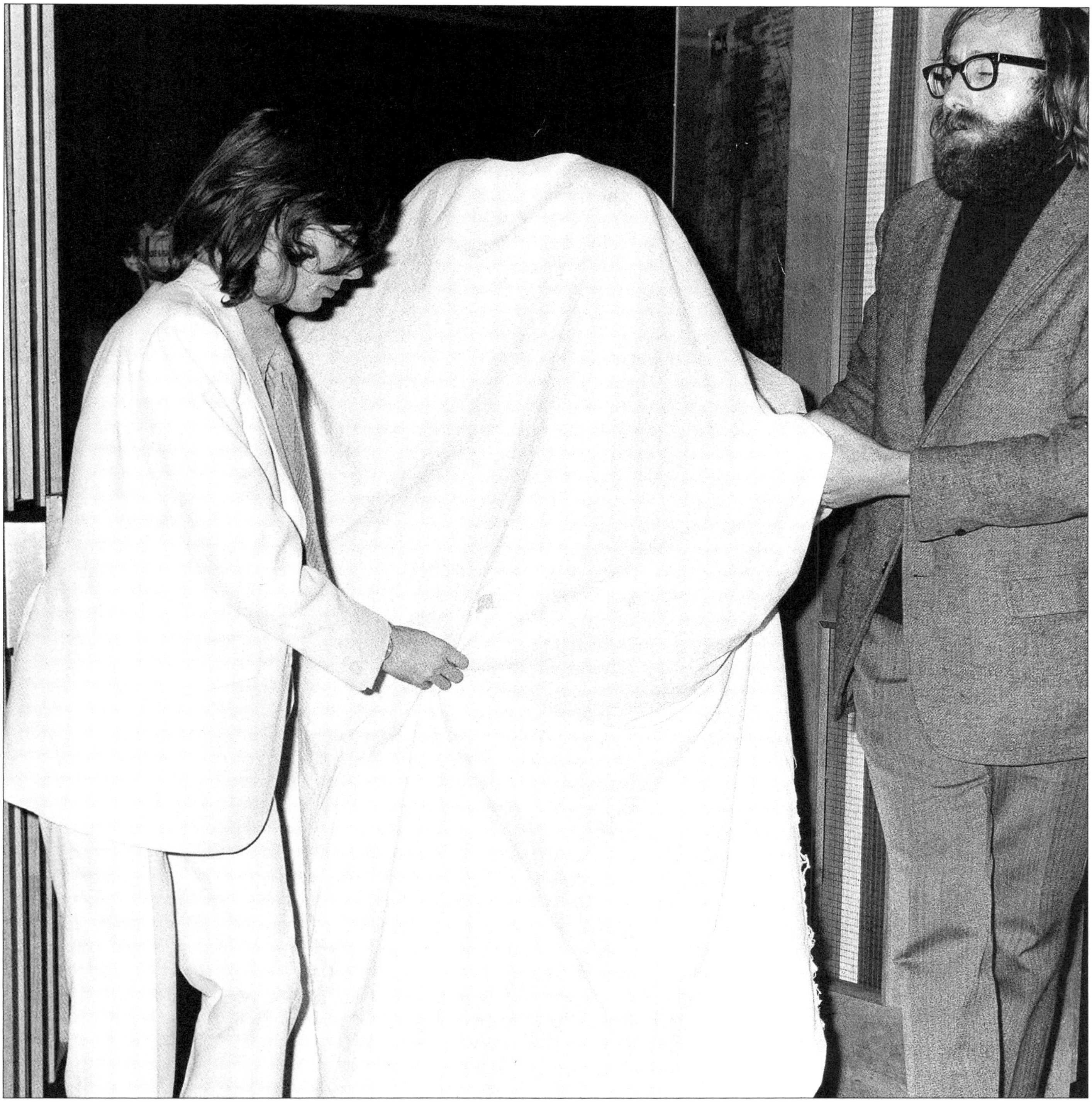

Car accident

Opposite: In July John and Yoko visit Liverpool and Scotland with Kyoko and Julian, but a car accident in Sutherland in Scotland puts them all into hospital. John and Yoko are unable to attend the Press launch of the *The Plastic Ono Band* and they fly back to London with sutures in their facial injuries.

Above: An evening of John and Yoko's movies is held at the ICA, London, on September 10. Movies shown included *Smile*, a slowed down film of John smiling, and their controversial *Rape*. Throughout the event a couple, believed to be John and Yoko themselves, sit on the stage in a white bag.

Chin Up!

A slightly sullen-looking John takes tea with Yoko having lost his beard for a while, supposedly at Yoko's request.

As The Beatles begin to disintegrate as a band, and John's relationship with Paul descends into legal argument, so John and Yoko become a tighter unit, occupying themselves with their own film and music projects, and their continued staging of 'happenings' and protests. On his way to perform at a hastily arranged Plastic Ono Band concert in Toronto, Canada, John decides privately to quit The Beatles.

Dear Harold

Returning the MBE

As part of his continued anti-war protests, John returns his MBE to the Queen. The title itself is irrevocable, but John returns the medal to Buckingham Palace with a letter detailing his reasons, including the government's stance on Nigeria and Vietnam, and the poor chart performance of his latest single. Ironically the decision provokes as much scorn as when he received the honour, not least from his Aunt Mimi who telephones immediately to reprimand him. Mimi, having treasured the item, had returned it to John unaware of his intentions.

Opposite: John holds up his letter at the Apple offices. A copy was also sent to the Prime Minister, Harold Wilson, who had originally recommended that The Beatles receive the award.

Drawing attention to the peace movement

John explained to the Press that he had always felt uncomfortable about accepting the MBE, but that he had done so as a Beatle because it was expected and he felt obliged to. Now he was rejecting it to draw attention to his peace movement - and the reference to his record was a joke, so the Queen wouldn't think his letter was from 'some boring colonel'.

MURDERED
HANRATTY

The Hanratty Cause...

John and Yoko took up another cause in December 1969, announcing plans to make a movie about the case of James Hanratty who had been hanged for murder in 1962. Irregularities in the case had gone part of the way to ensuring the end of capital punishment in Britain.

Left and below: John and Yoko meet the parents of James Hanratty.

BRITAIN
MURDERED
HANRATTY

Continuing the protest

John and Yoko continue their protest over Hanratty's death outside the Kensington Odeon in London, where Ringo's latest movie, *The Magic Christian*, is opening.

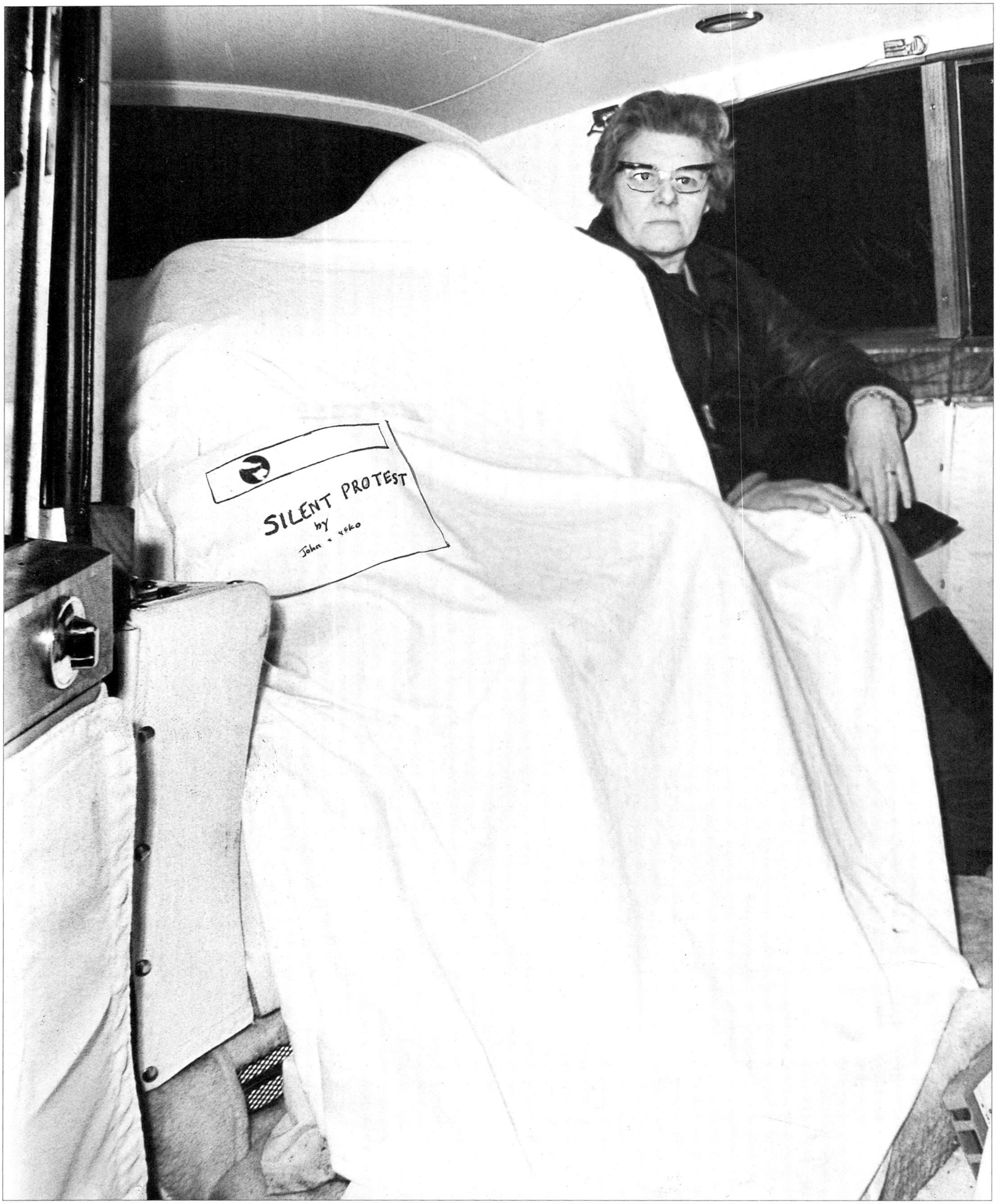
SILENT PROTEST
by
John + Yoko

'War is Over'

Opposite: A few days later, John and Yoko attend a speech made by James Hanratty's father at Speakers' Corner, Hyde Park, during which he declares his son's innocence. They stand in silent protest inside a white bag bearing the words, 'Britain Murdered Hanratty', and a petition is later handed in at Downing Street. Mary Hanratty, James's mother, sits next to John and Yoko in John's white Rolls-Royce.

Above: On December 15 The Plastic Ono Band played their second concert at the Lyceum Ballroom London in aid of the charity UNICEF. The line-up included Keith Moon, Eric Clapton and Billy Preston, alongside John and Yoko, performing in front of a backdrop which read, 'WAR IS OVER'.

John Lennon and the Plastic Ono Band...

Seeking to expand his musical horizons as The Beatles crumbled around him, John had pursued his ideas of conceptual music with Yoko Ono. The *Get Back* project had been hellish for him, and it proved to be the final nail in The Beatles' coffin. The process of putting together Beatles albums had become not just laborious but suffocating, and John sought a new spontaneity, a rawness and vitality which The Beatles as a group could no longer achieve. He needed a new outlet and he found it in the form of the Plastic Ono Band.

A conceptual band

The original idea behind the Plastic Ono Band was purely conceptual; a band without members - 'some pieces of plastic and a tape recorder', as John put it. In fact, at the launch party, with John and Yoko hospitalized in Scotland, this was precisely the form the band appeared in. However, the first recording that John credited to 'The Plastic Ono Band' was 'Give Peace A Chance', taped at the 'bed-in' in Montreal, and the first live performance was given in Toronto, John having assembled a group of musicians literally overnight.

Artistic freedom

In practise the Plastic Ono Band took the form of a loose assembly of musician friends, centered around John and Yoko, but including Keith Moon, Eric Clapton, and sometimes George and Ringo. The band allowed John a greater degree of artistic freedom than he could possibly have hoped for as a Beatle, for no one quite knew what to expect from them, and it also fulfilled John's desire for quickly recording and releasing music.

Cold Turkey

Their second single was 'Cold Turkey', a painfully honest account of John's attempts to withdraw from heroin, and a song which The Beatles did not feel comfortable with issuing. December 12 heralded the release of the band's first LP, a recording of their debut performance entitled *Live Peace In Toronto.*

Opposite: John and Yoko leave London for Canada on a Christmas peace crusade. Whilst in Ottawa they have a private conference with Canadian Prime Minister Pierre Trudeau.

Man of the Decade

At the end of the year, John is featured in ITV's three-part program, *Man of the Decade*, along with John F. Kennedy and Mao Tse Tung.

CHAPTER EIGHT

Early Seventies Nothing's gonna change my world

In January 1970, when Paul, George and Ringo came together in the studio to record George's song 'I, Me, Mine' for the album *Let It Be*, John was not there with them. He was with Yoko in Denmark, from where he announced that all the proceeds from his music would in future be used to promote peace. He had now almost totally turned his attention away from The Beatles and towards what he was doing with Yoko, particularly in the areas of conceptual and avant-garde art. Later in the month an exhibition of his lithographs, *Bag One*, opened at the London Arts Gallery, featuring a series of erotic pictures depicting him and Yoko on their honeymoon. Almost immediately the exhibition was raided and closed down by the police, and eight pictures were confiscated for being obscene. However, just over three months later the courts decided that the pictures were not indecent after all, and they were all returned. John and Yoko did not come back from Denmark until the end of January, when they appeared in London with their hair cropped short. They later gave their tresses to Michael X in return for a pair of Muhammad Ali's boxing shorts, which they planned to auction to raise money for their peace campaign.

The Plastic Ono Band was still releasing records - and even appeared on BBC television's *Top of the Pops*, performing a recently released single, 'Instant Karma'. In keeping with John's belief that music should be more immediate, 'Instant Karma' had been both written and recorded within the space of just one day.

In March, John revealed to the French magazine, *L'Express*, that he and the other Beatles had smoked cannabis in the toilets at Buckingham Palace, before they were presented with their MBEs in 1965. The same month he broadcast a message to a CND rally in London, during which he mentioned that Yoko was pregnant for the third time. Unfortunately, yet again she lost the baby.

To all intents and purposes, the rifts within The Beatles were still not public knowledge, but in April, in a Press release for his album, *McCartney*, Paul effectively said he was leaving the group. For years afterwards

Paul was blamed for precipitating the break-up, when actually he had been the last to go. However, John was furious - he had been talked out of making public his decision to leave, and now Paul had beaten him to it. He bitterly resented Paul appearing to be the decision-maker, just as he had resented him trying to lead The Beatles after Brian Epstein's death.

In his personal life, despite his fulfilling and exciting partnership with Yoko, John found he was still having problems that he felt dated back to his troubled childhood. During this period he was introduced to the work of Dr Janov, who proposed a therapy called 'primal scream' to cure neurosis. He and Yoko went through a course of this therapy with Janov himself, which certainly seemed to help John come to terms with a great many of his hang-ups, and led to him writing his soul-baring songs such as 'Mother' and 'God'. The therapy also precipitated a massive argument about the events of his childhood with his father, who had come to see John at Tittenhurst Park with his wife. It was the last time John saw Fred, although he did speak with his father again on the phone before Fred died in 1976 - by which time John was living permanently in America.

Several of John's continuing worries were to do with the business affairs of The Beatles. Their contractual arrangements were in a mess, and Allen Klein discovered that, despite what they had been led to believe, *Yellow Submarine* did not constitute the third in their three-movie contract with United Artists. Fortunately there was enough material from *Get Back*, their abortive documentary, to make a full-length feature movie instead. The revised project, now called *Let It Be*, was sold to UA and was premièred in New York in May 1970 - none of The Beatles attended.

Although The Beatles as a group were officially no more, with each member set on a solo career, the four of them were still legally tied together until 1975 by The Beatles & Co, the company they had formed three years earlier. Under the terms of their agreement, all the income any of them made, even from their solo albums, was to be split four ways. At the end of December 1970, Paul decided he had had enough of abortive discussions with the others and he filed a lawsuit in London, seeking dissolution of The Beatles & Co and the appointment of a receiver to sort out the group's affairs. The High Court case was heard in London during February and March 1971 and Paul, supported by his wife, Linda, was the only Beatle to attend. It soon became apparent that Klein's company had taken at least $500,000 more than they were entitled to, and the judge finally ruled in favor of Paul.

Meanwhile, John and Yoko had become deeply involved in movie making, and in creating avant-garde art films. After *Rape* they made *Erection* - although its title may have led the audience to expect something different, this actually showed the progress of a hotel being erected in London over a nine-month period. Two of their films, *Apotheosis (Balloon)* and *Fly*, were premièred at the Cannes Film Festival in May 1971. *Apotheosis (Balloon)* simply showed a balloon taking off from a field, while the soundtrack of everyday noises fades away to silence.

Although Yoko's divorce from Anthony Cox had been reasonably amicable, in 1971 he vanished with Kyoko. John and Yoko believed that he had taken her to New York, so in June they flew to America to look for her. They later returned to England for a few months, during which they attended the signing for the official release of *Grapefruit*, Yoko's book that previously had only been available in a limited edition. They also made their last public appearance in the UK, when they were both interviewed on the *Parkinson* show on network television. In September they returned to New York for a short visit, which turned into a permanent stay. Part of the reason was that Yoko soon started legal proceedings to win custody of Kyoko, but they also decided they felt more comfortable in New York. Yoko had spent a great deal of time there when she was younger, and she showed John round and introduced him to her favorite haunts. The Press in Britain had ridiculed them and their beliefs, and had made fun of Yoko as an artist, but in America they seemed less critical and more open to new ideas.

Towards the end of 1971, John released one of his most critically acclaimed solo albums, *Imagine*, which topped the charts in both Britain and America. The songs were gentler - more commercial and less avant-garde - than those he had released previously. However, he also included a bitter attack on Paul in a song called 'How Do You Sleep?' in answer to several songs on Paul's LP, *Ram*, which had included some rather pointed lyrics against John and Yoko. Now that it was out in the open, the fight continued in public. In an interview with *Melody Maker* in November 1971, Paul complained that he just wanted to sort out their business problems between the four of them, but that John was refusing to meet. John's letter of reply was published two weeks later. It was a bitter attack on Paul, pointing out that he had been the one to instigate the lawsuit and that they couldn't just sort out the business between themselves as there were ongoing problems with the taxman to resolve. It was to be four years before the two of them met again, in New York, and even then the animosity between them was still not fully resolved.

Meanwhile, John was settling into his new life in New York. At the end of October he was a guest artist at Yoko's exhibition, *This Is Not Here*, and later that month, he and Yoko invited the children of the Harlem Community Choir to join them to record 'Happy Christmas (War Is Over)'. It was released as a single in the US at the beginning of December, and quickly became a classic Christmas song - although it was nearly a year later before it was available in the UK.

They also still continued to work for peace and against injustice - in December they appeared at a benefit rally for writer John Sinclair, who had been imprisoned in 1969 for ten years, for possession of a very small amount of marijuana. He was released on bail just over two days later. However, both John and Yoko's US visas were about to expire - and by now the US authorities had begun to realize that John would continue speaking out on controversial issues and that his views would be listened to and respected by a wide range of people.

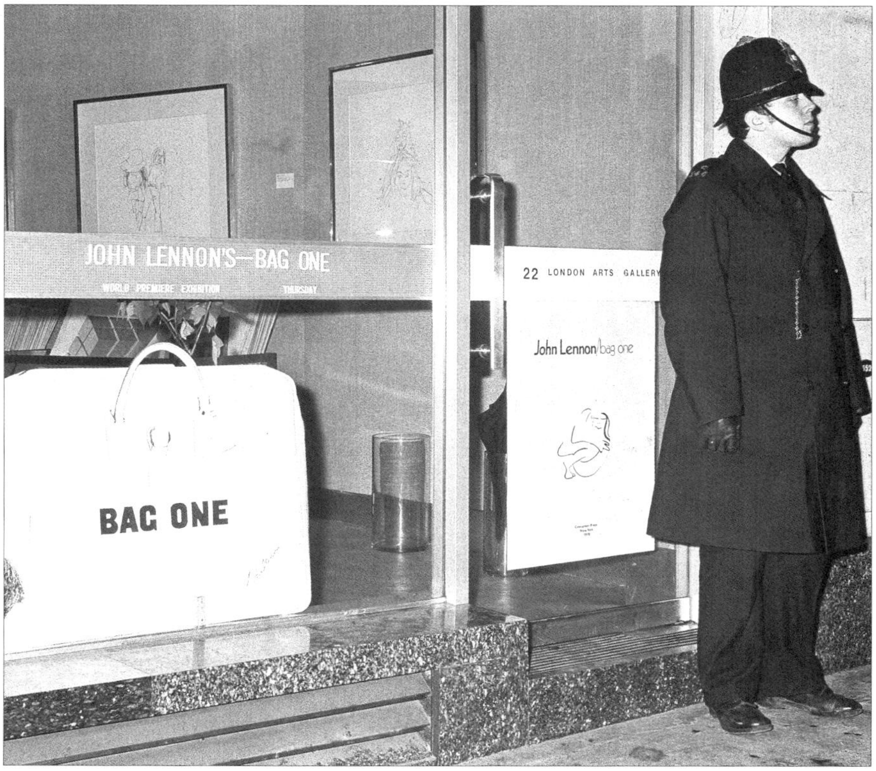

Previous pages: Yoko and John on their way to Canada..

Right: Police stand guard outside John's exhibition of lithographs, *Bag One*, at the London Arts Gallery.

Bag One

On returning from Canada, John and Yoko travel to Denmark for Christmas and New Year. Whilst there, John's exhibition, *Bag One*, opens in London. It features a series of erotic pictures depicting him and Yoko on their honeymoon, so it is temporarily closed by police the following day, with eight lithographs confiscated on the grounds of obscenity. Sales of John's prints reportedly soar following the police raid.

Below and opposite: John and Yoko continue their campaign with a Christmas message, displayed on billboards in eleven different cities around the world. It reads: 'WAR IS OVER! IF YOU WANT IT. Happy Christmas from John & Yoko'.

WAR
IS
OVER!
IF YOU WANT IT
Happy Christmas from John & Yoko

Cananda

Opposite and below: John and Yoko stay on a farm just outside Toronto during their visit to Canada, where they meet with the entertainer and civil rights campaigner Dick Gregory.

Left: Inside the London Arts Gallery at John's exhibition, a police photographer takes pictures of the offending exhibits. However, just over three months later the courts decide that the pictures are not indecent after all, and they are all returned.

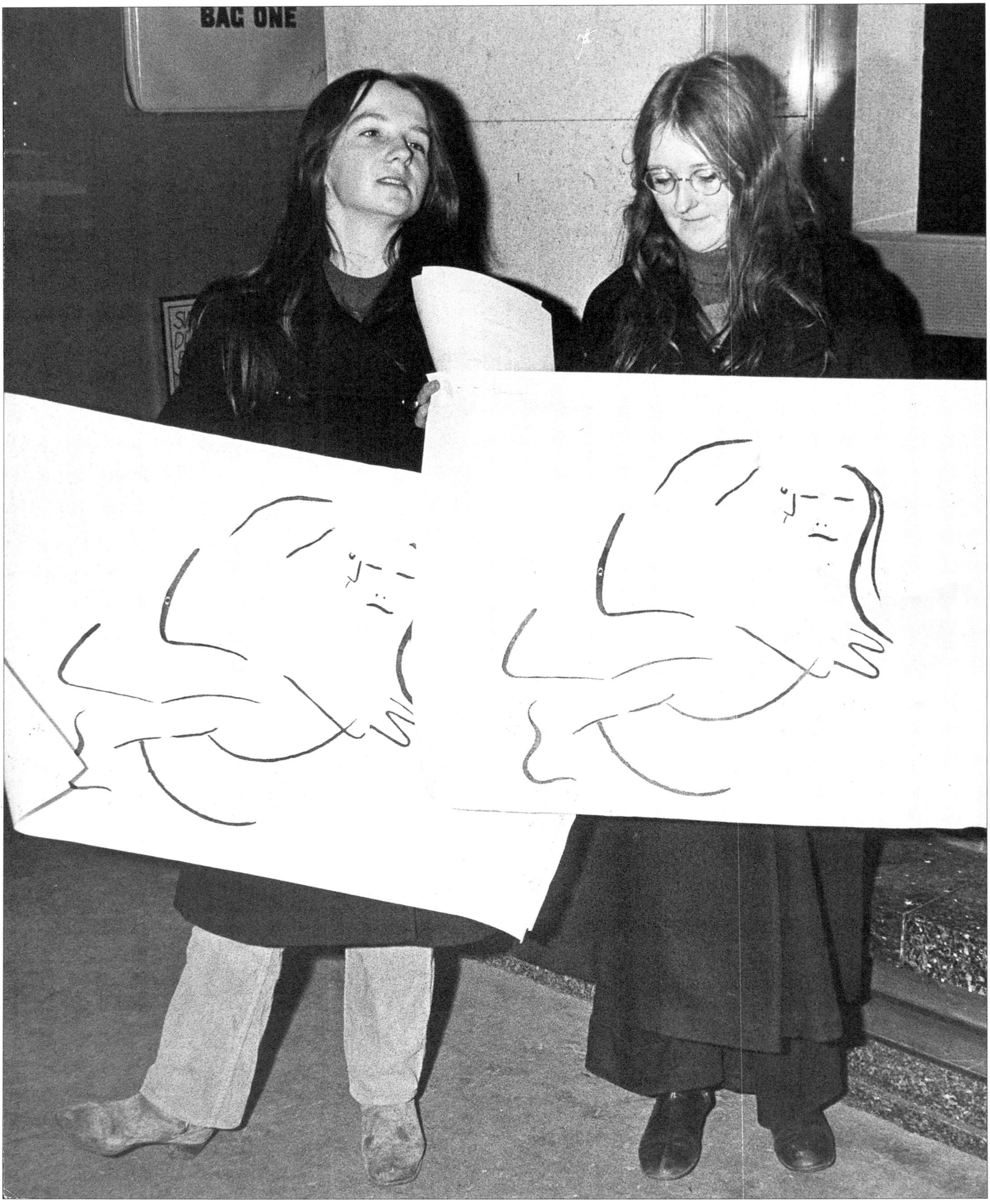
BAG ONE

Hair crop in Denmark

Above: John and Yoko spend Christmas and New Year in Alborg, Denmark, with Kyoko, at the home of Anthony Cox and his new wife. While there they have their hair cropped and later visit the peace center in Jutland.

Opposite: Sales of John's prints reportedly soar following the police raid.

Michael X

John and Yoko visit the civil rights campaigner Michael X, leader of the 'Black Power' organization at his headquarters in London's Holloway. They exchange their shorn hair for a pair of Muhammad Ali's bloodstained boxing shorts. Both items will be auctioned for peace causes later in the year.

Michael X

Previous pages: John removes his hat to reveal his new haircut. The crop is evidently a do-it-yourself job, carried out in the barn of Cox's Jutland home.

On the roof of the 'Black Power' headquarters in London, John, Yoko and Michael X show Ali's shorts and the shorn hair - neatly tied in a plastic bag - to the waiting Press.

Cynthia remarries

Opposite: On August 1, 1970, Cynthia marries Italian hotelier, Roberto Bassanini with Julian in attendance.

Above and previous pages: John and Yoko share a loving look.

Plastic Ono Band

Opposite: John and Yoko at Heathrow Airport on their way to Majorca in 1971 By 1970 The Beatles were effectively over, with John, Paul, George and Ringo all focusing on solo projects, John having released his first real solo album, *John Lennon / Plastic Ono Band* In December. There would be years of legal wrangling until the split was official, but proceedings begin in early 1971 to dissolve the group.

Above: Roberto Bassanini swings Julian into the air after the wedding.

Imagine

Paul's album, *Ram*, was soon to be released and it included some rather pointed lyrics against John and Yoko. Within five months John was to counter with *Imagine*, which included a bitter attack on Paul in a song called 'How Do You Sleep?'. However, in general the songs were gentler - more commercial and less avant-garde - than those he had released previously and the record topped the charts in both Britain and America.

Cannes Film Festival

In May 1971 John and Yoko travel to Nice, en route to the Cannes Film Festival where two of their films, '*Fly*' and '*Apotheosis (Balloon)*' are to be premièred.

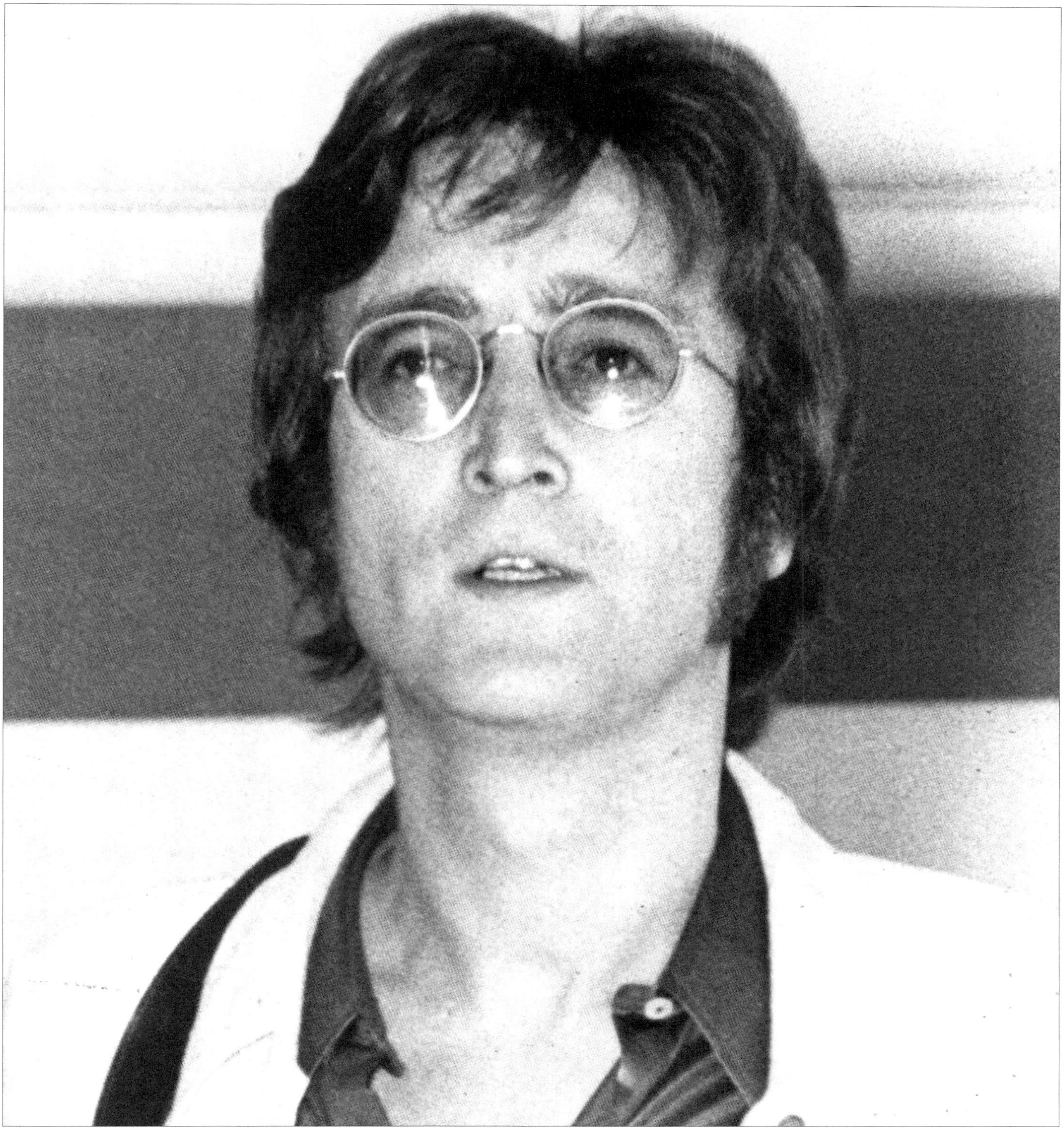

'Apotheosis (Balloon)'

Opposite: John looking pensive on the beach at Cannes. *Apotheosis (Balloon)* simply showed a balloon taking off from a field, while the soundtrack of everyday noises fades away to silence.

Above: John returning from the Festival.

DOOR

Custody battle

John is finally granted a nine-month US visa in the summer of 1971, and he and Yoko travel to New York in order to try and obtain custody of Yoko's daughter Kyoko. Whilst there John begins work on his Imagine album, completing recording at his Tittenhurst Park home studio in July. Later that month Yoko re-released her book *Grapefruit,* attending signings in New York and London with John at her side.

Opposite and above: John and Yoko arrive back in London from New York to publicize her book *Grapefruit*.

Working Class Hero

John and Yoko in 1971 promoting his single 'Working Class Hero' from the LP *John Lennon / Plastic Ono Band*. The words of the song revealed the pressures he had been under during his school years and were bitter and resentful about the 'system', which he felt had let him down badly. As a result of his recent experience with primal scream, many of John's songs during this period were written with searing honesty and are full of heart-rending emotion.

Apple Records
POWER TO THE PEOPLE
OPEN YOUR BOX

Grapefruit

John and Yoko were only in England for a few months, during which they attended the signing for the official release of *Grapefruit*. Yoko's book, which contained instructions such as 'Cut a hole in a bag filled with seeds and place the bag where there is wind', had previously only been available in a limited edition. They also made their last public appearance in the UK, when they were both interviewed on the BBC television show *Parkinson*.

Opposite: John and Yoko peer over a copy of Yoko's book at a signing in Selfridges, London.

GRAPEFRUIT
YOKO ONO

In America

On September 3, 1971, John and Yoko flew out for another visit to New York, as they continued their battle to gain custody of Kyoko. John would never again return to British soil. The couple took up residence in New York and continued to perform and record together throughout 1972.

Live in New York

John and Yoko perform together at a charity concert in New York's Central Park. In November, he and Yoko invited the children of the Harlem Community Choir to join them to record 'Happy Christmas (War Is Over)'. It was released as a single in the US at the beginning of December, and quickly became a classic Christmas song - although it was nearly a year later before it was released in the UK.

CHAPTER NINE

Life In America
Nobody told me there'd be days like these

Although 1972 began well, with John and Yoko demonstrating outside the BOAC building to support a boycott of UK exports as a protest against British policy in Northern Ireland, and hosting *The Mike Douglas Show* - on which John performed with Chuck Berry, one of his teenage idols - it quickly deteriorated. At the end of February both John and Yoko's US visas expired, although they were both granted routine temporary fifteen-day extensions to allow them to make fresh applications. Soon afterwards, Yoko was awarded custody of Kyoko, but before the child could be handed over her father took her into hiding. A few days later, both John and Yoko's temporary visa extensions were suddenly cancelled, and they were served with deportation orders, citing John's 1968 drugs conviction. Yoko immediately appealed, saying that they would lose custody of her daughter if they left America - even though Kyoko still had not been found. It was quickly apparent that John's drug conviction had little to do with what was happening - John and Yoko's friends in New York included a whole crowd of left-wing radicals and political activists, and the American government had taken note. Even the mayor of New York, John Lindsay, wrote to the immigration board to say that the real reason the couple were being deported was because they spoke out on issues of the day. Not long afterwards, during an appearance on *The Dick Cavett Show*, John claimed his privacy was being invaded by government agents. It was the beginning of his long battle against deportation - although Yoko was granted permanent residency in March 1973, at the same time John was ordered to leave the US within sixty days.

Despite the 1971 High Court ruling, The Beatles' joint business affairs took a long while to untangle. Allen Klein and ABKCO did not reach the end of their term as business managers of Apple and the other Beatles companies until the end of March 1973, and The Beatles & Co partnership was not formally dissolved until January 1975. The strain of all this, and of fighting the deportation order, had its effect on John and Yoko's marriage. John could be volatile and difficult to live with at the best of times; when he was under stress he retreated into himself and also tended to drink too much. Unfortunately, he couldn't handle alcohol - he often became abusive and sometimes violent. Towards the end of 1973 Yoko decided that time apart would do them both good and John went to Los Angeles with their secretary, May Pang. What was supposed to be a temporary separation turned into a fifteen-month 'lost weekend', as John settled into a house with Keith Moon and Ringo and the three of them over-indulged in both drink and drugs. May was good company and she looked after John well, but he still loved Yoko and missed her the entire time. However, Yoko would not allow him to return until she felt he had worked through some of his fantasies and hang-ups. John himself later referred to this period as a 'grow-up time'.

Meanwhile, he continued his fight against deportation, suing the US government over alleged illegal wiretapping and FBI surveillance, claiming in court that attempts to deport him were based on his involvement in anti-war demonstrations and not on his drug conviction, and requesting the right to question officials about an alleged police vendetta. He was ordered to leave the US again, but again he appealed. By now he was supported by many influential people in the US, and the groundswell of public opinion was firmly behind him. Despite everything else that was going on during this period, he did not neglect his music - he managed to produce two good albums, *Walls and Bridges, and Rock 'n' Roll.*

After Klein was accused of irregularities in his accounting, following one of George's concerts for charity, relations between all four Beatles were much improved. The others had to admit that Paul's fears about him had been justified and in November 1973 John, George and Ringo sued Klein for misrepresentation in the High Court. Paul and John began to communicate again, and Paul even visited John while he was in Los Angeles and the two played together.

In November 1974 John kept a promise to perform at Elton John's Thanksgiving Concert in New York, and met up with Yoko again backstage. Within a couple of months he had returned to live with her in New York - and they soon announced that she was expecting a baby. John's deportation was delayed because of the pregnancy, but the following month the order was finally reversed by the New York State Senate.

After their son, Sean, was born on John's thirty-fifth birthday, 8 October 1975, John announced he was taking five years off to focus on bringing up his child, while Yoko carried on working. They settled in New York permanently, and John was granted his Green Card in July 1976. This meant that he could safely leave the US without fear of being refused permission to return, so in June 1977, he, Yoko and Sean were able to go to Japan for five months to visit Yoko's family.

At the beginning of 1980, John and Yoko bought a seafront mansion in Florida, where they celebrated their eleventh wedding anniversary. Later that year, John went on holiday alone to Cape Town, South Africa, and soon afterwards he began to compose again.

Having almost completed the promised five years looking after Sean, John also began to record again and soon brought out a new album, *Double Fantasy*, just in time for his son's fifth birthday in October. The reviews were good and in public John seemed happy and full of enthusiasm. He began to move back into the public eye, doing a huge, three-week interview, along with Yoko, for *Playboy*, and shorter interviews for *Newsweek* and *Rolling Stone*, as well as radio interviews for BBC's Radio 1 with Andy Peebles and RKO radio.

Early on 8 December, as John came out of the Dakota building where he and Yoko lived in New York, he was stopped by Mark Chapman and signed a copy of Double Fantasy for him. Chapman then waited outside the building all day, until John returned home from the studio late that night. As John headed toward his home, five shots were fired at point-blank range. Although John was rushed to hospital, he was pronounced dead on arrival.

The sense of grief and outrage at his death was overwhelming all around the world, but was even more hysterical in America. In Britain there had been little news of him over the previous few years, but in America he had captured the hearts of those opposed to the war in Vietnam and had been known as an outspoken opponent of any kind of injustice. Many felt they had lost an inspirational leader. On 14 December Yoko called for ten minutes of silence to be observed at 7.00 p.m. GMT around the world in his memory, and throughout December the airwaves were full of the sound of 'Imagine', one of his best-loved songs.

In memory of John, a large area of New York's Central Park was renamed Strawberry Fields. At the site-opening ceremony in March 1984, attended by Yoko, Sean and Julian, Yoko revealed that it was where she and John had gone on their last walk together. She appealed for every country to send something for the planned garden, as a tribute to John. Many responded, and when the finished garden was opened in October 1985 it contained plants from all round the world.

One unexpected result of John's death was that the other three Beatles started collaborating again. Right back in the Seventies the four of them had planned to produce a documentary that would tell their story in their own words, tentatively titled *The Long And Winding Road.* The project had suffered the same fate as many others during their break-up - the four of them could never agree on how things should be done. Now the three remaining Beatles came together to produce a television documentary and three double albums, all entitled *The Beatles Anthology*. Paul, George and Ringo were interviewed for the project and John was included in the form of old interviews, mainly from his solo days. Yoko had sent them some tapes of John, including several unfinished songs, sparking off the idea that the three of them should finish them off. It was not so dissimilar to how they had worked in the old days, and toward the end of 1995 the first single, 'Free as a Bird', was released along with the television documentary. Newspapers ran whole pages devoted to the 'Fab Four', and magazines brought out special issues - even after twenty-five years The Beatles were big news.

In May 2002, twenty-two years after John's death, the readers of *The Guardian* newspaper took part in a Jubilee poll to establish the person who had done more to shape Britain during the fifty years of Queen Elizabeth II's reign than the Queen herself. The final list included politicians, entertainers and scientists; The Beatles came joint sixth, but the man who brought them together came in at number one. John Lennon may be gone, but in the hearts and minds of many all round the world he is certainly not forgotten.

The Lost Weekend

In October 1973 John split from Yoko after four and a half years of marriage, embarking on what has become known as his 'lost weekend'. The split was to last over a year, in which time John moved to LA with his secretary May Pang. John binged on drugs and alcohol with Keith Moon and Ringo throughout the separation but continued to release singles and recorded his album of rock n' roll classics with Phil Spector.

It was at this time that Paul and John began to communicate again, and Paul even visited John while he was in Los Angeles and the two played together.

In November '74 'Whatever gets you through the night' tops the billboard charts becoming Lennon's first solo US number one. Elton John played keyboards on the recording.

Below: John with May Pang in New York.

Right: John in Los Angeles during his 'lost weekend'.

Opposite: Back in New York City. John returned to stay with Yoko at the Dakota Building, New York, in January 1975. In the same month, The Beatles were formally dissolved.

Elvis

At the Dakota

Above: John on the roof of his apartment at the Dakota Building wearing a wool beret and an Elvis pin on his jacket.

Opposite: February 1975. John inside his apartment in the Dakota building New York. In March John announced that his 18 month separation from Yoko proved to be "not a success" and that they were once again to live with each other. Later that year, in October, Yoko gives birth to a son named Sean Tara Ono Lennon.

Lennon can stay in US

In July 1976 John's application for permanent residency in the US is approved, thus ending years of battle to remain in the country.

Right and previous page: John with Yoko at a party held in tribute to Lew Grade, owner of the rights to Northern Songs.

Below: Art Garfunkel, Paul Simon, Yoko Ono, John Lennon and Roberta Flack pose together backstage at the Grammy Awards, Uris Theater, New York City.

Opposite: John's father, Alfred Lennon, was to pass away in Brighton in 1976. John, having had very little contact with him throughout his life, did not return to England for the funeral.

Double Fantasy comeback

Soon after completing the promised five years looking after Sean, John began to record again, bringing out a new album, *Double Fantasy*, just in time for his son's fifth birthday in October. The reviews were good and in public John seemed happy and full of enthusiasm. He moved back into the public eye with a huge, three-week interview, along with Yoko, for Playboy, and shorter interviews for Newsweek and Rolling Stone, as well as radio interviews for BBC's Radio 1 with Andy Peebles and RKO radio.

Opposite: In a rare and poignant photograph taken just three months before his death, John Lennon signs an autograph for a fan, much as he was to do for Mark Chapman in December 1980.

CENTRAL PARK

EMPIRE

John Lennon killed

Early on 8 December, as John came out of the Dakota building he was stopped by Mark Chapman and signed a copy of Double Fantasy for him. Chapman then waited outside the building all day, until John returned home from the studio late that night. As John headed towards his home, Chapman fired five shots at point-blank range at him. Although John was rushed to hospital, he was pronounced dead on arrival.

Previous page: Almost as soon as the news of John's death is announced, distraught fans begin to gather outside the Dakota Building.

Opposite: Still mourning a few days after Lennon's death, around 20,000 fans gather in Liverpool to hold a candlelit vigil in St George's Square. Several such tributes take place across the world.

Above: Young fans crushed in the crowds at the memorial service. Over one hundred injuries were reported as crowds swelled in the small square.

Mourning a hero

Above: Police attempt to hold back the crowds at the memorial service in Liverpool.

Right: Mourning fans burn black candles.

Opposite: Fans in America, his home for the last few years of his life, where he had captured the hearts of those opposed to the war in Vietnam and had been known as an outspoken opponent of any kind of injustice, gather to grieve Lennon's death.The sense of grief and outrage at his death was overwhelming all around the world, but was perhaps more vividly expressed in America.

DAILY NEWS
JOHN LENNON
SLAIN HERE
Ex-Beatle shot; nab suspect
Killed outside his apartment
DO
CRUSS

CAN you
See How
STUPID
VioLence
is ?

OH,
UNTIMELY
DEATH...
JOHN LENNON 1940-1980
THANK YOU
JOHN

John Lennon's message

Hope, peace and love: five year old Paula Carney gets the message. In March 1981, 2000 fans gathered in Matthew Street at the site of the Cavern Club where the Beatles sound was born. Not far away another 2000 people packed the Anglican Cathderal for a festival of peace in his memory.

Overleaf: A poster in America claiming that John's Lennon's murder was a 'political assassination'. Lennon had been subject to FBI investigation throughout the US government's attempts to deport him. John's allegiances with civil rights campaigners and his anti-Vietnam stance were suggested that Lennon be considered as something of an undesirable.

One month after Lennon's death, *Double Fantasy* had sold more than one million copies and went simultaneously gold and platinum. 'Imagine' went to no 1 in the UK charts. It remained there for four weeks, only to be replaced by John's other single 'Woman'.

In the 6 weeks following his death, more than 2 million copies of Lennon records were sold in the UK alone. UK sales of 'Imagine' went on to pass the 1 million mark.

Cavern
PROUT comes

EVIDENCE SUBSTANTIATES THAT LENNON'S KILLER DID NOT ACT ALONE!! *(SEE BELOW)*
LENNON WAS KILLED ONE WEEK BEFORE A SCHEDULED APPEARANCE IN A LABOR STRIK
JOHN LENNON'S MURDER WAS A POLITICAL ASSASSINATION!
IT WAS BY NO ACCIDENT OR WHIM THAT JOHN LENNON'S ASSASSINATION CAME AT PRECISELY THE POINT WHEN LENNON RE-EMERGED INTO PUBLIC AND POLITICAL LIFE AFTER 5 YRS. OF SECLUSION FOLLOWING ATTEMPT TO DEPORT HIM!
ASSASSINATION INFORMATION COMMITTEE
DON'T MOURN-ORGANIZE!
POWER TO THE WORKING
LENNON ASSASSINATION WAS PART OF A PATTERN WITH CWP-5, MILK & MOSCONE, LOWENSTEIN, GARCIA, etc. AS U.S. GOVERNMENT ESCALATES PREVENTIVE ELIMINATION OF OPPOSITION!
JOHN LENNON'S ASSASSINATION WAS A CASE OF PREVENTIVE ELIMINATION OF POTENTIAL OPPOSITION AND AN ATTEMPT TO INTIMIDATE & DEMORALIZE THE MA WHO IDENTIFIED WITH LENNON AND THE ANTI-WAR MOVEMENT AS THE ROCKEFELLER-LED U.S. CAPITALIST CLASS & ITS SECRET POLICE (LED BY THE CENTRAL INTELLIGENCE AGENCY) SEEK TO PROMOTE A RIGHTWARD SHIFT POLITICS IN ORDER TO COUNTERACT THE NATURALLY OCCURRING LEFTWARD COMING ON THE HEELS OF THE MUTINY OF U.S. SOLDIERS IN VIETNAM (BLACKE IN ALL MEDIA), THE HEROIC VICTORY OF THE VIETNAMESE PEOPLE OVER U.S. CAPITALISM-IMPERIALISM, THE WATERGATE PERIOD, AND THE WIDESPREAD RECOGNITION OF THE ECONOMIC-SOCIAL-POLITICAL FAILURES OF CAPITALISM! DOMESTICALLY AND WORLDWIDE!
IT'S ALWAYS A LONE NUT-A WACKO!? *
EVIDENCE SUBSTANTIATES THAT CHAPMAN WAS NOT ACTING ALONE
A CHAPMAN PROGRAMMER-DR. JULES BERNHARDT &
MARK DAVID CHAPMAN-A PROBABLE C.I.A. MIND CONTROL SUBJECT

POLICE
DEPARTMENT

Father's footsteps

Above: Singer songwriter Julian Lennon in December 1984. His debut album *Valotte* reaches number twenty in the UK and seventeen in the US.

Previous page: One year on, fans gather in Liverpool for the first anniversary of John Lennon's death.

Opposite: March 1986. Yoko Ono arrives at Heathrow Airport with her son Sean, in advance of concerts in Wembley as part of her '*Star of Peace*' Tour.

Giving peace a chance

Right: March 1986, Yoko Ono and son Sean in London for her '*Star of Peace*' tour which will take in 33 cities in seven weeks.

Below: Yoko Ono on stage at Wembley.

John Lennon's legend continues

At the end of the twentieth century the readers of both *Mojo* magazine and *Q* magazine voted John Lennon the greatest rock star of all time.

In May 2002 a jubilee poll to establish the person who had done the most to shape Britain during the fifty years of Queen Elizabeth II's reign put John Lennon at Number One. John Lennon may be gone, but in the hearts and minds of many all round the world he is certainly not forgotten.

John Lennon: Chronology

1940

Oct 9 John Winston Lennon is born to Julia and Alfred Lennon at the Oxford Street Maternity Hospital, Liverpool. Alfred is absent.

1941

John is primarily cared for by his aunt and uncle, Mary (Aunt Mimi) and George, at 251 Menlove Avenue, Woolton.

1942

Apr John's father leaves home, having been away at sea for much of the time since his son's birth. Julia moves in with a new boyfriend, John Dykins.

1945

Sept John attends school at Dovedale Primary, Liverpool.

1946

Jul John is taken to Blackpool by his returning father, who intends to keep his son in his custody. Julia eventually locates the pair, and John decides to return to his aunt Mimi's in Liverpool.

1952

Jul John leaves primary school.

Sept John attends Quarry Bank High School with childhood friend Pete Shotton.

1955

5 Jun John's Uncle George dies aged 52.

1955

Skiffle music is popularized by Lonnie Donegan, and John's interest leads to the acquisition of his first guitar.

1957

March John forms The Blackjacks skiffle group, soon to be renamed The Quarry Men.

24 May The Quarry Men make their debut public performance at a street carnival, Roseberry Street, Liverpool.

9 Jun The Quarry Men fail to qualify for Carroll Levis' TV Star Search, held at the Empire Theatre, Liverpool.

Jul John leaves Quarry Bank High School.

6 Jul John meets Paul McCartney for the first time, when The Quarry Men play at St Peter's church summer fete.

20 Jul Paul joins The Quarry Men.

7 Aug The Quarry Men perform their debut at Liverpool's Cavern Club.

Sept John enrols at Liverpool College of Art, where he is to meet his future wife, Cynthia Powell, and future Beatle, Stuart Sutcliffe.

1958

6 Feb George Harrison joins The Quarry Men, having watched them perform at Wilson Hall, Liverpool.

15 Jul John's mother Julia is killed by a an automobile whilst crossing the road outside Aunt Mimi's house.

1959

29 Aug — The Quarry Men perform at the opening of the Casbah coffee club, run by the mother of The Beatles future drummer, Pete Best.

15 Nov — Johnny and the Moondogs, with John, Paul and George, make the final audition for TV Star Search.

1960

10 May — The Quarry Men become The Beatals.

20-28 May — The group tour Scotland in a support slot as The Silver Beetles.

2 Jun — They perform at Neston Institute as The Beatles.

Jul — John leaves art college.

August — The Beatles secure a stint in Hamburg, Germany, playing grueling sets at the Indra and the Kaiserkeller, where they meet Ringo Starr.

5 Dec — John returns to Liverpool after four months in Hamburg. George had been deported shortly before, for being under-age, and Paul and Pete Best were asked to leave having been accused of starting a fire.

1961

9 Feb — The group play their first Cavern Club gig as The Beatles, performing in a lunchtime slot.

21 Mar — The Beatles' first evening performance at the Cavern Club.

Apr — The Beatles return to Hamburg. Stuart Sutcliffe leaves the group to focus on his art studies.

Jun — 'My Bonnie', a single by Tony Sheridan, is released in Germany, featuring backing by The Beatles.

6 Jul — John contributes an article, 'Being a Short Diversion on the Dubious Origins of Beatles', to the first edition of Liverpool music paper Mersey Beat.

1 Oct — John and Paul holiday in Paris for two weeks.

28 Oct — Local record-shop owner, Brian Epstein, learns of The Beatles' existence from fans enquiring about 'My Bonnie'.

9 Nov — Brian Epstein attends a Beatles' performance at the Cavern Club.

Dec — Brian Epstein offers to manage The Beatles, John accepts on their behalf.

1962

1 Jan — The Beatles audition for Decca in London, recording fifteen tracks. Although the audition is to prove unsuccessful, Brian Epstein is later to use the recordings to cut a demo for EMI.

24 Jan — The Beatles sign a management contract with Brian Epstein, although at this stage Epstein does not sign himself.

8 Mar — The Beatles make their radio debut, recording at the Playhouse Theatre, Manchester, for BBC radio's Teenager's Turn (Here We Go.

10 Apr — Former Beatles' bassist, John's close friend Stuart Sutcliffe, dies of a brain hemorrhage in Hamburg, at the age of twenty-one.

13 Apr — The Beatles make their third trip to Hamburg, securing a residency at the new Star-Club until the end of May.

9 May — Brian Epstein secures a contract for The Beatles with Parlophone, a subsidiary of EMI. He notifies the group, who are in Hamburg, with a congratulatory telegram.

4 Jun — Brian and the Beatles are signed to EMI, recording their first session at Abbey Road studios two days later.

15 Aug — Ringo Starr, drummer with Rory Storm and the Hurricanes (who had also built something of a reputation through playing in Hamburg), is invited to join The Beatles as it is suggested that Pete Best lacks sufficient skill for recording work. Best is fired the following day.

18 Aug — Ringo joins The Beatles, making his debut at Hulme Hall, Port Sunlight.

23 Aug — John marries Cynthia Powell at Mount Pleasant Register Office, Liverpool. Cynthia is pregnant.

4 Sept The Beatles return to Abbey Road for their first formal recording session. Ringo is present, but due to an oversight, producer George Martin had invited session drummer Andy White, and subsequently it was White who was to drum on the first single, 'Love Me Do'.

1 Oct Brian Epstein signs a five-year management contract with The Beatles.

5 Oct 'Love Me Do', backed with 'P.S. I Love You' is released as The Beatles first single.

17 Oct The Beatles make their television debut, performing live on the regional Granada program People and Places.

26 Nov The Beatles record their second single, 'Please Please Me'.

1963

11 Jan Release of 'Please Please Me'.

19 Jan The Beatles make their national television debut, on Thank Your Lucky Stars.

11 Feb The Beatles record their first album in one eleven-hour session.

22 Feb Formation of Northern Songs'; publishers of all future Lennon- McCartney songs.

2 Mar 'Please Please Me' is at the top of the Melody Maker chart, and at the number one position on at least two other charts. The album of the same name is to go to number one later in the month.

8 Apr John becomes a father as Cynthia gives birth to a son, John Charles Julian Lennon.

11 Apr Release of 'From Me To You', The Beatles' third single. It is to be the first of eleven consecutive single releases to top the British chart, through to 1966.

28 Apr John goes on holiday to Spain with Brian Epstein.

21 Jun The Daily Mirror reports that John Lennon had beaten up Cavern Club DJ, Bob Wooler, on 18 June , at Paul's 21st birthday party. Wooler was apparently hospitalized by Lennon after suggesting that he was having an affair with Epstein.

29 Jun John's first solo television appearance on BBC's Juke Box Jury.

3 Aug The Beatles perform for the last time at the Cavern Club.

23 Aug UK single release of 'She Loves You'/ 'I'll Get You'.

4 Nov John utters his celebrated '...rattle your jewelry' witticism at The Royal Variety Performance , Prince of Wales Theatre, London.

29 Nov UK single release of 'I Want To Hold Your Hand'/ 'This Boy'.

27 Dec John and Paul are described as 'the outstanding English composers of 1963' in The Times.

1964

Jan — The Beatles embark upon a low-key French tour. They are informed by a telegram from Capitol Records in New York of their first US number-one single, 'I Want To Hold Your Hand'.

9 Feb — The Beatles perform on The Ed Sullivan Show in the US.

11 Feb — The Beatles play their first concert in the US, at the Washington Coliseum.

2 Mar — The Beatles begin shooting their first movie, A Hard Day's Night'.

20 Mar — UK single release of 'Can't Buy Me Love'/ 'You Can't Do That'.

23 Mar — The Beatles are presented Carl-Alan awards by The Duke of Edinburgh.

23 Mar — 'In His Own Write', John's first book, is published. The first print-run quickly sells out.

4 Apr — The Beatles occupy the top five positions of the American singles chart.

23 Apr — John attends a Foyle's literary luncheon, held in his honor. John declines to make a much-hoped-for speech.

6 Jul — The Beatles' movie A Hard Day's Night premieres in London.

10 Jul — UK single release of 'A Hard Day's Night'/ 'Things We Said Today'.

10 Jul — A civic reception is held in Liverpool to honor The Beatles.

15 Jul — John and Cynthia buy a mansion,'Kenwood, in Weybridge, Surrey.

18 Aug — The Beatles leave London for their first major US tour.

28 Aug — The Beatles are introduced to Bob Dylan, who in turn introduces them to marijuana.

27 Nov — UK single release of 'I Feel Fine'/ 'She's A Woman'.

1965

9 Jan — John appears on Peter Cook and Dudley Moore's Not Only...But Also program, reading his poetry.

15 Feb — John passes his driving test aged 24.

9 Apr — UK single release of 'Ticket To Ride'/ 'Yes It Is'.

11 Jun — It is announced at midnight that The Beatles are to receive MBEs. Two days later several members return their MBEs in protest.

24 Jun — John's second book, A Spaniard In The Works is published.

23 Jul — UK single release of 'Help'/ 'I'm Down'.

29 Jul — The Beatles second movie Help!, premieres in London.

3 Aug — John buys his Aunt Mimi a bungalow in Dorset.

15 Aug — The Beatles' second US tour opens at New York's Shea Stadium to a record audience of 55,600.

26 Oct — The Beatles receive their MBEs at Buckingham Palace.

3 Dec — UK single release of 'We Can Work It Out'/ 'Day Tripper'.

3 Dec — UK album release of Rubber Soul.

31 Dec — John's father, Alfred, releases his first and only single, 'That's My Life (My Love And My Home)' to a poor response.

1966

4 Mar — The Evening Standard publishes an interview with John, reported by Maureen Cleave, in which he states that The Beatles are 'more popular than Jesus'.

10 Jun — UK single release of 'Paperback Writer'/ 'Rain'.

29 Jul — The Maureen Cleave interview is published in US teen magazine Datebook.

31 Jul — Radio stations in the US 'Bible Belt' ban The Beatles, and bonfires of their records and memorabilia are organized as a reaction to John's comments.

5 Aug — UK single release of 'Eleanor Rigby'/ 'Yellow Submarine'.

6 Aug — Brian Epstein holds a press conference in New York to explain John's 'Jesus' comments.

11 Aug — The Beatles fly to Chicago for the start of what is to prove their final US tour.

12 Aug — Supported by the rest of the group, John faces the American Press to explain and apologize for his remarks.

29 Aug — The Beatles make their last stage appearance at San Francisco's Candlestick Park.

5 Sept — John goes to Celle in West Germany to begin filming his part in How I Won the War, where he is to acquire his trademark spectacles.

9 Nov — John meets the conceptual artist Yoko Ono at her exhibition, Unfinished Paintings and Objects, at the Indica Gallery, London.

27 Nov — John films a sketch for Not Only...But Also, to be broadcast on Christmas Day.

1967

17 Feb — UK single release of 'Strawberry Fields Forever'/ 'Penny Lane'. It fails to reach the top of the chart.

26 May — The Beatles' ground-breaking album Sgt. Pepper's Lonely Hearts Club Band is released ahead of the official date of 1 June..

25 Jun — The Beatles perform 'All You Need Is Love' on the world's first global satellite television link-up.

24 Jul — John, Paul, George, Ringo and Brian Epstein sign a Times published petition calling for the legalization of marijuana.

24 Aug — John, George and Paul, with wives and friends, attend a lecture given by the Maharishi Mahesh Yogi in London, traveling to a weekend seminar in North Wales the following day.

27 Aug — Brian Epstein is found dead at home in bed, London.

11 Sept — Shooting begins on The Beatles' next movie, Magical Mystery Tour.

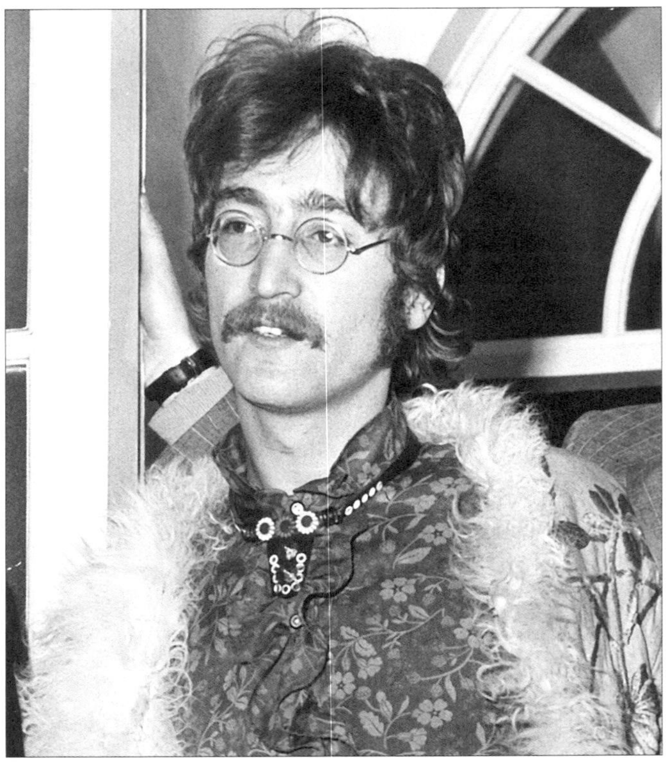

30 Sept John and George appear on appear on ITV's The Frost Programme with the Maharishi.

11 Oct Yoko plus Me, an exhibition at London's Lisson Art Gallery is anonymously sponsored by John.

18 Oct How I Won the War premieres at the London Pavilion.

5 Oct John and George attend the opening party for The Beatles' Apple Boutique.

16 Dec John and George attend a UNICEF gala in Paris with the Maharishi.

26 Dec The BBC premieres Magical Mystery Tour (in black and white) to a great deal of public criticism.

1968

5 Jan John is visited at his Weybridge home by his father, who seeks John's blessing in marrying nineteen-year-old Pauline Jones.

25 Jan John and George attend an Ossie Clark fashion show in London. George's wife Pattie is amongst the models.

15 Feb John, Cynthia, George and Pattie fly to Rishikesh in India to study meditation for three months with the Maharishi Mahesh Yogi.

12 Apr John, Cynthia, George and Pattie arrive back in London.

11 May John and Paul go to New York for five days, where they announce the establishment of their Apple business venture.

14 May John denounces the Maharishi on NBC's The Tonight Show and announces the formation of Apple Corps.

22 May John and Yoko Ono appear together in public for the first time, attending a party and Press conference for another Apple Boutique.

15 Jun John and Yoko participate in the National Sculpture Exhibition by planting two acorns outside Coventry Cathedral; it marks their first 'event'.

18 Jun John attends the opening of In His Own Write with Yoko, the play having been adapted by actor and friend, Victor Spinetti, from John's two books.

21 Jun Apple Corps buys premises on Savile Row, London.

1 Jul You Are Here, John's first art exhibition, opens in London with the release of 365 balloons.

22 Aug Cynthia sues John for divorce, on the grounds of his affair with Yoko Ono.

18 Oct A police raid takes place at 34 Montagu Square, London, an apartment owned by Ringo, where John and Yoko are staying. The pair are charged with obstructing the police and with possession of cannabis.

25 Oct John and Yoko announce that Yoko is pregnant, the child is expected in February the following year.

8 Nov John and Cynthia are divorced.

21 Nov Yoko miscarries her child and John stays with her at Queen Charlotte's Maternity Hospital, Hammersmith, London.

28 Nov John pleads guilty to possession of cannabis, whilst charges against Yoko are dropped. John is fined £150 and twenty Guineas costs. Both are found not guilty of obstruction.

29 Nov John and Yoko's first album, Unfinished Music No 1 - Two Virgins, sees its UK release.

10 Dec John's home, Kenwood, is put up for sale.

11 Dec John takes part in the Rolling Stones' 'Rock and Roll Circus', which remains uncompleted.

18 Dec John and Yoko appear inside a white bag at the Royal Albert Hall, London, as part of Alchemical Wedding, a party hosted by the underground art movement.

23 Dec Apple holds its Christmas party at Savile Row, where John and Yoko hand out gifts dressed as Santa Clause and Mother Christmas.

1969

3 Jan 30,000 copies of Two Virgins are confiscated in New Jersey on the grounds that the sleeve photography is pornographic.

18 Jan Apple's financial difficulties are revealed by John in an interview with Disc and Music Echo's Ray Coleman.

30 Jan The Beatles perform together for the last time on the roof of the Apple building, London. The event is filmed as part of the Let It Be project.

2 Feb Yoko Ono is divorced from her husband Anthony Cox.

3 Feb Allen Klein is brought in to deal with The Beatles' finances, despite opposition from Paul.

2 Mar John and Yoko make an appearance at an avant-garde jazz performance in Cambridge.

20 Mar John and Yoko are married at the British Consulate in Gibraltar. They spend just over an hour there before flying back to Paris.

24 Mar John and Yoko meet Salvador Dali in Paris, for lunch.

25 Mar John and Yoko begin a week-long 'bed-in' at the Amsterdam Hilton, Holland.

31 Mar John and Yoko fly to Vienna to launch their movie Rape, which is premiered on television that night. They appear in a white bag for a brief Press conference at the Hotel Sacher.

1 Apr John and Yoko appear on Thames Television's Today program.

21 Apr John and Yoko's film and production company, Bag Productions, is formed.

22 Apr John changes his middle name to Ono at an official ceremony on the roof of the Apple building.

4 May John and Yoko buy their Berkshire mansion, Tittenhurst Park.

9 May John and Yoko's second album, Unfinished Music No 2 - Life With The Lions, is released in the UK, on the newly formed Zapple label.

16 May John's 1968 drug conviction brings about the rejection of his application for a US visa.

26 May John and Yoko begin their second 'bed-in' at the Queen Elizabeth Hotel, Montreal, Canada.

1 Jun 'Give Peace a Chance' is recorded during the 'bed-in' by'The Plastic Ono Band, a makeshift group which includes John, Yoko and their friends, including guests such as Timothy Leary.

1 Jul John, Yoko, Yoko's daughter Kyoko and Julian are involved in a car crash in Scotland, and hospitalized until 6 Jul.

3 Jul — Perspex tubes, fitted with microphones, tape recorders and amplifiers stand in for the still hospitalized John and Yoko, at the launch of The Plastic Ono Band in London.

4 Jul — John's first solo single, 'Give Peace a Chance', is released, credited to The Plastic Ono Band.

22 Aug — The last photograph of all The Beatles together, is taken at John and Yoko's home, Tittenhurst Park.

1 Sept — John, Yoko, George, Pattie, Ringo and Maureen (Ringo's wife), see Bob Dylan play at the Isle of Wight festival.

10 Sept — The New Cinema Club holds an evening of John and Yoko's films, at the ICA, where a couple, possibly John and Yoko, sit on stage throughout, contained within a white bag.

13 Sept — John decides to quit The Beatles whilst on his way to a hastily arranged concert in Toronto with The Plastic Ono Band; his decision, however is not made public.

Oct — John meets his father for the last time, at Tittenhust Park.

12 Oct — Yoko has a second miscarriage at King's College Hospital, London. John resumes his use of heroin, which he had been attempting to stop.

24 Oct — The Plastic Ono Band release 'Cold Turkey' as a UK single.

3/10 Nov — Nash House, London, holds two nights of John and Yoko's films, under the title Something Else.

7 Nov — John and Yoko release their Wedding Album in the UK in a luxurious package.

13 Nov — John Lennon offers a tiny island, Dornish, rent-free to a group of hippies.

25 Nov — John returns his MBE to Buckingham Palace, in protest against government policy over Nigeria, military action in Vietnam, and the poor chart performance of his latest single.

10 Dec — John and Yoko meet the parents of James Hanratty, a convicted murderer, who was hanged in 1962. They plan to make a movie proving his innocence.

11 Dec — John carries a banner outside the premiere of Ringo's The Magic Christian, proclaiming, 'Britain Murdered Hanratty'.

12 Dec — The Plastic Ono Band release the LP Live Peace in Toronto, worldwide.

14 Dec — John and Yoko protest silently, inside a white bag, at Speakers' Corner, Marble Arch, over the hanging of Hanratty. Later a petition is handed to 10 Downing Street.

15 Dec — John and Yoko appear with the Plastic Ono Band, featuring Yoko, Eric Clapton, Billy Preston and Keith Moon, at a UNICEF charity concert, at the Lyceum Ballroom, London.

23 Dec — John and Yoko have a private conference with Canada's Prime Minister, Pierre Trudeau in Ottawa, Canada.

24 Dec — John and Yoko briefly join a sit-in in Kent.

29 Dec — John and Yoko fly to Denmark to holiday with Kyoko, her father Anthony Cox and his wife Melinda.

30 Dec — John is featured in a three -part program on ITV, Man of The Decade, with John F. Kennedy and Mao Tse Tung.

1970

3/4 Jan — Paul, George and Ringo record together for Let It Be, their last recording session in John's lifetime. John is absent.

5 Jan — John makes the announcement that all proceeds from his music will in future be used to promote peace.

15 Jan John's exhibition of lithographs, Bag One, opens in London.

16 Jan Bag One is closed as police confiscate eight lithographs depicting John and Yoko, for reasons of obscenity.

20 Jan John and Yoko have their hair cropped in Denmark.

22 Jan John's lithographs go on show in the US at Detroit's London Gallery.

27 Jan John writes and records 'Instant Karma'.

4 Feb John and Yoko swap their recently shorn hair for a pair of Mohammed Ali's boxing shorts with Michael X, leader of Black Power. They intend to auction them to raise money for peace causes.

6 Feb John and Yoko release 'Instant Karma'/ 'Who Has Seen The Wind?' in the UK.

12 Feb The Plastic Ono Band perform 'Instant Karma' on the BBC's Top of The Pops.

22 Mar John reveals in an interview with L'Express, a French magazine, that the Beatles smoked cannabis in the toilets at Buckingham Palace in 1965.

29 Mar A message is broadcast at a CND rally in London, in which John reveals Yoko is pregnant for a third time.

10 Apr Paul publicly announces his resignation from The Beatles.

23 Apr John and Yoko go to LA for a course of primal scream therapy.

27 Apr John's lithographs are returned, after a court decides that they are not indecent.

8 Dec John interviewed by Rolling Stone. The interview is published in two parts in early 1971, and later, as 'Lennon Rems'.

11 Dec The LP John Lennon / The Plastic Ono Band is released worldwide.

31 Dec Paul begins proceedings to end the partnership of The Beatles.

1971

19 Feb The hearing to dissolve The Beatles & Co. Partnership commences in the London High Court.

12 Mar John and Yoko release 'Power To The People'/ 'Open Your Box' as a single in the UK.

12 Mar The High Court judge rules in Paul's favour.

15 May Two of John and Yoko's films, 'Apotheosis (Balloon)' and 'Fly', premiere at the Cannes Film Festival.

31 May John is granted a nine month US visa.

1 Jun John and Yoko fly to New York to try to locate Kyoko, and to gain custody of her.

6 Jun John meets Frank Zappa, later appearing live with Yoko, and Zappa's band 'The Mothers of Invention' at New York's Fillmore East.

Jul John records the album 'Imagine', mostly at his 'Tittenhurst Park' home.

15 Jul John and Yoko attend a signing, promoting the re-publication of Yoko's 'Grapefruit'.

17 Jul John and Yoko make their last UK public appearance, interviewed on 'Parkinson'.

11 Aug John and Yoko are amongst demonstrators in London, supporting anti internment in Northern Ireland, and the Oz magazine editors who are being tried for obscenity.

3 Sept John and Yoko fly to New York. The 'visit' becomes a permanent stay.

9 Sept John appears on The Dick Cavett Show', explaining the disbanding of the Beatles.

8 Oct The LP 'Imagine' sees its UK release.

9-27 Oct John is a guest artist at Yoko's 'This Is Not Here' exhibition in New York.

6 Nov John and Yoko appear at a benefit in New York after demonstrations over the 'Attica Prison' riots.

1 Dec 'Happy Christmas (War Is Over)' is issued as a single in the US (24th November. 1972 in the UK).

4 Dec John attacks Paul in the 'Melody Maker's' letters page.

11 Dec John and Yoko appear at a rally for writer John Sinclair who was imprisoned in 1969 for ten years on charges of marijuana possession. He is released on bail just over two days later.

1972

5 Feb John and Yoko participate in protests supporting a boycott of British exports against policy in Northern Ireland.

14-18 Feb John and Yoko host 'The Mike Douglas Show'. John performs with Chuck Berry, a teenage idol of his.

29 Feb John and Yoko's US visas expire.

3 Mar Yoko is awarded custody of Kyoko, but Kyoko's father takes her into hiding.

6 Mar John and Yoko's temporary visa extensions are canceled.

16 Mar John is served with a deportation order which cites his 1968 drug conviction.

22 Apr — John and Yoko protest against US action in Vietnam at the National Peace Rally, in New York.

29 Apr — An announcement is made of a written appeal from the mayor of New York City, John Lindsay, which calls for the deportation orders against John and Yoko to be dropped.

11 May — John appears on 'The Dick Cavett Show' claiming that his privacy is being invaded by government agents.

12 Jun — John and Yoko release their double LP, 'Sometime In New York City' in the US (15th September in the UK).

30 Aug — John and Yoko stage two charity concerts in New York at Madison Square Gardens.

23 Dec — John and Yoko's film 'Imagine' premieres on US television.

1973

23 Mar — John is ordered to leave the US within sixty days, whilst Yoko is granted permanent residency. John formally appeals the following day.

Oct — John embarks upon his 'lost weekend', separating from Yoko and flying to LA with their secretary, May Pang.

24 Oct — John sues the US government over alleged FBI surveillance.

Oct-Dec — John records a rock and roll album produced by Phil Spector.

2 Nov — John, George and Ringo sue Allen Klein for misrepresentation in the High Court. Klein counter-sues.

2 Nov — US release of LP 'Mind Games' and 'Mind Games'/ 'Meat City' single (16 November. in the UK).

1974

13 Mar — John is thrown out of the 'Troubadour' night-club for disrupting a 'Smothers Brothers' concert.

27 Mar — A complaint against John, made by a waitress from the 'Troubadour' is dismissed by the LA district attorney.

17 Jul — John is again given sixty days to leave the US.

31 Aug — John claims that attempts at his deportation center around his involvement in anti-war demonstrations, rather than his drug conviction.

23 Sept — John releases 'Whatever Gets You Through The Night'/ 'Beef Jerky' as a single in the US (4th Oct. in the UK).

26 Sept — John releases his 'Walls And Bridges' LP in the US (4th Oct. in the UK).

28 Oct — Allen Klein loses his court case to John, Ringo and George.

16 Nov — John has his first US solo No.1 with 'Whatever Gets You Through The Night'. Elton John plays keyboards on the track.

28 Nov — John sings three songs with Elton John at Madison Square Garden.

16 Dec — John issues '#9 Dream'/ 'What You Got' as a US single (31st Jan. 1975 in the UK).

27 Dec — John, Julian and May Pang holiday in Disneyland.

1975

Jan — John records with David Bowie.

Jan — John returns to Yoko in New York.

9 Jan — The Beatles & Co. are formally dissolved in the London High Court.

17 Feb — John's LP 'Rock 'n' Roll is released in the US (21st Feb. in the UK).

6 Mar John issues a statement that his separation from Yoko is over.

10 Mar The single 'Stand By Me'/ 'Move Over Mrs L', is released in the US (18th Apr in the UK).

13 Jun John gives his last performance before an audience, on 'A Salute To Lew Grade', television special.

23 Sept John's deportation is delayed due to Yoko's pregnancy.

7 Oct The deportation order which John has been fighting for some years, is reversed by the New York State Senate.

9 Oct Sean Taro Ono Lennon is born to John and Yoko on John's thirty-fifth Birthday.

24 Oct 'Working Class Hero' is released in the UK only.

1976

5 Jan The Beatles former tour manager, Mal Evans, is shot dead by police in LA.

26 Jan The Beatles recording contract with EMI expires, Paul stays with EMI, George and Ringo move to other labels, and John does not sign with anyone.

1 Apr John's father, Fred, dies in hospital in Brighton, England.

27 Jul John finally receives his Green Card.

Oct John decides to retire from music in order to focus on bringing up Sean.

1977

10 Jan All outstanding litigation is settled with Allen Klein.

20 Jan John and Yoko attend the inauguration of Jimmy Carter as president in Washington DC.

4 Apr The Beatles attempt to stop the release of an LP recorded in Hamburg in 1962, but fail.

Jun John, Yoko and Sean go to Japan for five months.

1978

4 Feb John and Yoko buy land in Delaware County, and are revealed to be buying several other apartments in the Dakota building where they are residents.

16 Jun John attempts to prevent *The News of The World* from publishing extracts from his first wife, Cynthia's book, 'A Twist Of Lennon', but is unsuccessful.

1979

27 May John and Yoko place adverts in newspapers in London, Tokyo and New York, entitled 'A Love Letter From John And Yoko, To People Who Ask Us What, When And Why'.

15 Oct $1000 is donated by John and Yoko to help to provide bullet-proof vests for the New York police.

31 Dec Various ventures which were established in the late Sixties are dissolved, including John and Yoko's film and production company, 'Bag Productions'.

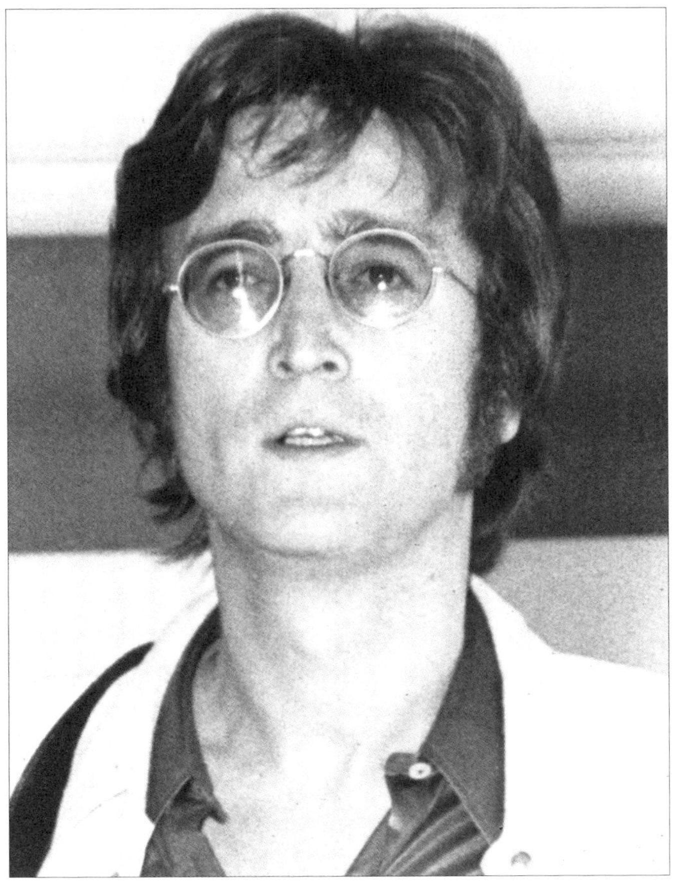

1980

28 Jan — John and Yoko buy a seafront mansion in Florida.

20 Mar — John and Yoko celebrate their eleventh anniversary in Florida. Yoko gives John a vintage Rolls Royce.

23 May — John holidays alone in Cape Town, South Africa.

Jul — John begins to compose again, in Bermuda.

4 Aug — John and Yoko begin studio work for a new album at the 'Hit Factory' studio, Manhattan.

9 Sept — John and Yoko begin a huge interview for 'Playboy', lasting almost three weeks.

22 Sept — Yoko signs a recording contract for herself and John with the newly formed independent label, Geffen Records.

29 Sept — 'Newsweek' publishes the first interview with John and Yoko to appear in several years.

9 Oct — Yoko has a message sky-written for John's fortieth birthday and Sean's fifth.

27 Oct — John releases the single '(Just Like) Starting Over'/ 'Kiss Kiss Kiss' in the US (24th Oct. in the UK).

17 Nov — John and Yoko release the album 'Double Fantasy'.

5 Dec — John records an interview with 'Rolling Stone' magazine.

6 Dec — John and Yoko record an interview together for BBC's Radio 1, with Andy Peebles.

8 Dec — John and Yoko record an interview with RKO Radio.

8 Dec — (9 Dec in the UK) John is shot and killed outside the Dakota apartment building in New York.

10 Dec — John is cremated at Hartsdale Crematorium, New York State.

14 Dec — Ten minutes silence is observed around the world, at 7pm GMT, in memory of John.

14 Dec — Extracts from the RKO interview are broadcast in the US.

20 Dec — '(Just Like) Starting Over' goes to No.1 in the UK, having previously slipped down the charts from 8th to 21st position.

27 Dec — '(Just Like) Starting Over' reaches the No.1 spot in the US, where it is to remain for five weeks. 'Double Fantasy' tops the album chart.

1981

12 Jan — US release of John's 'Woman'/ 'Beautiful Boy (Darling Boy)' (16th Jan. in the UK).

18 Jan — Yoko responds to the messages of goodwill which she has received since John's death, by publishing a letter of gratitude in newspapers around the world.

18 Jan — Radio 1 broadcasts the first of five programs entitled 'The Lennon Tapes', airing the Andy Peebles interview of the sixth of December 1980.

20 Feb — Yoko's only UK solo single, 'Walking On Thin Ice' is released. She is interviewed on radio for the first time since John's death.

Mar — An announcement is made that a forest is to be planted in Israel as a tribute to John.

Mar — Paul publishes his tribute, which includes previously unseen photographs taken by his wife Linda.

13 Mar — US release of 'Watching The Wheels'/ 'Yes I'm Your Angel' (27 March. in the UK).

29 Mar — A memorial service for John is held in Liverpool.

11 May — George releases a tribute single, 'All Those Years Ago', featuring Paul and Ringo, in the US (15th May in the UK).

22 May — Yoko makes her first official public appearance since John's death, accepting the 'Handel Medallion', New York's highest cultural accolade.

24 Aug — John's murderer Mark Chapman is sentenced jailed for a minimum term of twenty years, and a maximum of life imprisonment.

9 Oct — Yoko proclaims this date, which would have been John's birthday, 'International World Peace Day'. A statue of John is unveiled in LA.

28 Oct — 'Lennon' the musical opens in Liverpool.

22 Dec — Sotheby's hold the first major rock memorabilia auction in London, selling a small Lennon self-portrait for £8000.

1982

Jan — The complete transcript of the extensive 'Playboy' interview is published in book form.

24 Feb — Yoko and Sean attend the Grammy awards, collecting the best album award for 'Double Fantasy'.

20 Apr — An official ceremony is held in Central Park, New York, where Yoko announces the planning of a three and a half acre site to be dedicated to John, named 'Strawberry Fields'.

1 Nov — 'The John Lennon Collection', a compilation album, is released in the UK (8th Nov. in the US).

13 Nov — The first annual 'John Lennon Scholarship' is awarded by George Martin on Behalf of The Performing Rights Society.

15 Nov — EMI release 'Love' as a single.

1983

1 Sept — The original hand-written lyrics for 'Imagine' are sold at Sotheby's for £6500.

11 Sept — The Peace Museum in Chicago exhibits a number of John's artifacts.

13 Oct — John is posthumously awarded the Freedom of the City by Liverpool City Council.

5 Dec — The LP 'Heart Play - Unfinished Dialogue', featuring John and Yoko's 1980 'Playboy' interview is released in the US (16 December. in the UK).

1984

5 Jan — US single release of 'Nobody Told Me'/ 'O' Sanity' (9th Jan. in the UK).

19 Jan — US album release of John and Yoko's 'Milk And Honey' (23rd Jan. in the UK).

13 Feb — Pete Shotton publishes 'John Lennon: In My Life', an account of his friendship with John.

9 Mar — UK single release of 'Borrowed Time'/ 'Your Hands' (11th May in the US).

15 Mar — US single release of 'I'm Stepping Out'/ 'Sleepless Night' (15th Jul in the UK).

21 Mar — Yoko officially opens the 'Strawberry Fields' site in Central Park with Julian, Sean and mayor Ed Koch.

Apr — An unauthorised double album, 'Reflections And Poetry' is released in the UK, containing part of the interview which John Gave to RKO before his death. Yoko takes legal action and the album is withdrawn.

Jun — Jon Weiner's 'Come Together: John Lennon In His Time' is published, in which Weiner discusses Lennon's previously withheld FBI files.

5 Oct — The single 'Every Man Has A Woman Who Loves Him', backed by Sean Lennon singing 'It's Alright', is released in the US (16th Nov. in the UK).

1985

13 May — John's uncle Charles unveils a new British Rail engine named 'John Lennon', for the London to Liverpool route.

9 Oct — Yoko and Sean open a garden on the 'Strawberry Fields' site, Central Park, New York.

2 Nov — The stage play 'Lennon' opens in London.

18 Nov — 'Jealous Guy' is issued by EMI as a single.

6 Dec — A collection of John's hand-written letters and lyrics go on display in the manuscripts room of the British Museum, on loan from Beatles biographer, Hunter Davies.

1986

24 Jan — US release of LP 'John Lennon: Live In New York City' (24th Feb. UK).

21 Mar — Yoko appears at Wembley Conference Centre, London, as part of her 'Star Peace Tour'.

6 Oct — A book of John's previously unreleased writings and drawings are published, entitled 'Skywriting By Word Of Mouth'.

27 Oct — US release of LP 'Menlove Avenue', containing previously unreleased recordings by John (3rd Nov. in the UK).

8 Dec — Czech police disperse hundreds of fans gathered for a public memorial service to John in Prague.

1987

4 Apr — The first 'John Lennon New Age Award' is awarded to promoter Bill Graham at the New York Music Awards, presented by Yoko.

24 Apr — A ballet based upon the album 'John Lennon / The Plastic Ono Band', entitled 'The Dream Is Over' premieres in London.

1988

20 Jan — The Beatles are added to the Rock and Roll Hall of Fame at an award ceremony held at the Waldorf Astoria in New York. George, Ringo, Yoko, Julian and Sean attend.

11 Jul — UK only release of 'The Last Word', consisting of part of the interview with John at RKO.

19 Sept — The preview of 'Imagine', a new Lennon art exhibition, is attended by Yoko at London's Business Design Centre.

30 Sept — Yoko unveils John's star on the Hollywood Walk of Fame, outside the Capitol Records building.

4 Oct — US release of CD/LP 'Imagine: John Lennon' (10th Oct. in the UK).

28 Oct — The documentary film 'Imagine: John Lennon' premieres in London. Three years were spent making the film which was authorised by Yoko, and as such, the producers had been granted unlimited access to the Lennon Estate's collection of footage, much of which had been previously unseen by the public.

1989

Jul — 'The Murder Of John Lennon' is published by Fenton Bresler, a British journalist and barrister, in which he claims CIA involvement in John's assassination.

Sept — Bag One Gallery is opened by Yoko Ono in New York, selling expensive 'official' Lennon merchandise.

1990

25 Mar — The Amsterdam Hilton re-opens room 209 on the 21st anniversary of John and Yoko's 'bed-in' there. The room is given the title, 'The John and Yoko Honeymoon Suite'.

1 Oct — A CD boxed set of John's songs from 1969 - 1980 is released by EMI as 'Lennon'.

9 Oct The 50th anniversary of John's birth is marked by a ceremony at the New York United Nations Building, featuring a short speech by Yoko, a recording of John talking about peace, and the playing of 'Imagine'. The event is broadcast live, world-wide.

7 Dec The 10th anniversary of John's death, and the 50th anniversary of his birth, are honoured in Liverpool by the lord mayor unveiling the first official plaque for John in his hometown.

14 Dec UK release of 'Testimony', a longer version of the RKO interview.

1991

Jan With impending military action by the UN against Iraq, 'Give Peace A Chance' is recorded by Yoko and Sean with Lenny Kravitz. The single is released in the UK on the 28th, but is met by a BBC ban.

20 Feb A 'Lifetime Achievement Award' granted posthumously to John, is collected by Yoko at the 33rd Grammy Awards ceremony.

12 Jul The FBI is instructed by a US court to release sixty-nine documents concerning John Lennon, which it had previously withheld on the grounds of 'national interest'.

6 Dec John's Aunt Mimi dies aged eighty-eight, at the Dorset home bought for her by John in 1965.

1992

15 Jul A new Lennon musical opens in Liverpool, also titled 'Imagine'.

Oct The play 'Looking Through A Glass Onion - John Lennon In Words And Music', runs in London for just a few days.

5 Oct 'The John Lennon Video Collection' is released by a subsidiary of EMI.

1993

17 Apr Yoko holds an exhibition in LA which includes a replica, in bronze, of the broken spectacles that John was wearing when he was killed.

1994

Jan John is posthumously entered into The Rock and Roll Hall of Fame in New York as a solo artist by Paul McCartney. During a Press conference with Paul and Sean, Yoko gives Paul a copy of the unfinished song 'Free as a Bird', with the intention that it may be completed by the remaining Beatles, to be included in 'The Beatles' Anthology', Apple's new CD and television project.

30 Nov A double Beatles CD, 'Live At The BBC' is released by EMI. Six million copies are sold within six months.

1995

Feb 'Real Love', a second unfinished Lennon composition is completed by Paul, George and Ringo.

19 Nov 'The Beatles Anthology' premieres on US television and includes the new 'Beatles' track 'Free as a Bird'.

21 Nov Release of 'The Beatles Anthology 1.', the first in a series of three double albums of unreleased out-takes and mixes.

4 Dec 'Free as a Bird' is released as a single, reaching No.2 in the UK charts.

1996

4 Mar 'Real Love' is released as a single.

18 Mar 'The Beatles Anthology 2.' is released.

28 Oct 'The Beatles Anthology 3.' Is released.

1997

20 Jun Yoko collects a posthumous award for John in London, recognising his outstanding contribution to British music.

25 Sept Eighty pages from the FBI's Lennon files are released as The American Civil Liberties Union, representing author Jon Weiner, win their case. Weiner is later to publish his findings in his book, 'Gimme Some Truth: The John Lennon FBI files'.

27 Oct Release of CD/LP 'Lennon Legend: The Very Best Of John Lennon' (23rd Feb. 1998 in the US).

1998

2 Nov UK release of the four CD set 'The John Lennon Anthology', containing over 100 previously unreleased tracks (3rd Nov. in the US).

1 Dec Yoko briefly revives the campaign she and John began in 1969, unveiling a 'War Is Over' poster in Times Square, New York.

1999

Apr John Lennon is voted 'the greatest rock singer of all time' in a 'Mojo' magazine readers' poll.

1 Aug John Lennon is ranked at number one in a 'Q Magazine' readers' poll, of the top '100 Greatest Stars of The 20th Century'.

Credits

Pictures in this book are copyright of Associated Newspapers,
except for the following which are copyright of the Hulton Getty Picture Archive.

(T = Top; B = Bottom; L = Left; R = Right):

1; 3; 7; 12; 16; 18; 19; 22; 24; 25; 31; 36; 37 - T + B;
60; 62; 66 – T; 77; 78 – T + B; 79;
113; 133 – T; 136; 141 – T; 142; 143; 148 – L + R; 149;
152; 159; 160; 163; 164 – B; 165; 166; 167 – T + B;
171; 173; 174; 177; 181; 184;
193; 196; 200; 203; 205; 206; 207 T + B;
217; 224; 225; 236; 241; 243; 244; 246;
250; 251; 252; 255; 257 – B; 268
273; 287; 304 – B; 305; 307; 310;
311; 327; 328; 329;
332 – T; 334; 335; 336; 337; 338;
342 – B; 343; 344; 345; 348 – B; 349;
350; 351; 352; 353; 357 – T, BL + BR;
364; 367 – TL, TR + BR

Bibliography

The Beatles, H. Davies (Arrow, London, 1992)
The John Lennon Encyclopedia, B. Harry (Virgin, London, 2000)
We All Shine On, P. Du Noyer (Carlton Books, London, 1997)
The Complete Beatles Chronicle, M. Lewisohn (Hamlyn, London, 2000)
Icons of Rock, A story in Photographs, T. Burrows (Bookmart, London, 2000)
Lennon, The Definitive Biography, R. Coleman (Pan, London, 2000)
Let Me Take You Down, J. Jones, (Virgin, London, 1993)
Last Interview, All We are Saying, D. Sheff, (Pan, London, 2001)